THE INTERPRETERS

RITUAL, VIOLENCE AND SOCIAL REGENERATION IN THE WRITING OF WOLE SOYINKA

THE INTERPRETERS

RITUAL, VIOLENCE AND SOCIAL REGENERATION
IN THE WRITING OF WOLE SOYINKA

Hakeem Bello

KRAFT BOOKS LIMITED

Published by

Kraft Books Limited
6A Polytechnic Road, Sango, Ibadan
Box 22084, University of Ibadan Post Office,
Ibadan, Oyo State, Nigeria
✆ +234803 348 2474, +234805 129 1191
E-mail: kraftbooks@yahoo.com
Website: www.kraftbookslimited.com

First published 2014

ISBN 978–978–918–195–7 (Paperback)
978–978–918–196–4 (Hardback)

First printing, July 2014

ACKNOWLEDGEMENTS

The core of this work comes from my undergraduate long essay at the University of Ilorin and the dissertation I submitted to the University of Ibadan in partial fulfillment of the requirements of a Masters degree in the 1989/90 session. Of course, a sustained interest in literature and my fascination with the intriguing life and works of the great writer and Nobel Laureate, Professor Wole Soyinka meant keeping in touch with that subject even as I made forays into journalism, rising to become the Editor of the now in limbo DAILY TIMES; and the public service by virtue of the kind appointments offered me first as Senior Special Assistant on Media and later Special Adviser on Media by the Governor of Lagos State, Mr Babatunde Fashola (SAN).

However, I am heavily indebted to Almighty God and so many people without whose input this book might probably not have been published.

First, I would like to thank Wumi Raji who served as my editorial consultant on this project. Wumi readily agreed to read through the manuscript that I produced out of the two projects and did not hesitate to declare it "publishable" after having gone through it. He also assisted in editing and proof-reading the work. I am really grateful to this reliable friend who also happened to be my senior at the University of Ilorin.

I must thank my boss, the Governor of Lagos State, Mr Babatunde Fashola (SAN) whose intellectual disposition cannot but infect anyone working with him. For their fraternal cooperation, I also thank my colleagues in the Lagos State Government's information management team, Mr Lateef Ibirogba and Mr. Lateef Raji.

Most grateful I am to my parents, Mr Moshood Bello and Mrs Sadiat Bello both of blessed memory for their valiant efforts as parents. I thank my brother and sisters led by Mrs Bolanle Tunji. My Uncles – Alhaji Taoheed Bello paid my way through school and Alhaji Tajudeen Bello gave me guardianship in Lagos from a rather tender age. I owe a debt of gratitude to my guardians in Ilorin, Dr and Mrs Lateef Oladimeji.

For the book itself, I am deeply grateful to my supervisors, Dr Bayo Ogunjimi, an unrelenting task master now of blessed memory for the B.A Project and Professor Albert Olu Ashaolu whose probing eyes and questions meant you should do more. I am equally grateful to my lecturers at both University of Ilorin and University of Ibadan, especially Professor Olu Obafemi.

I was particularly inspired and remain so till date by my Stylistics lecturer later at the University of Ibadan, Professor Niyi Osundare (*Aigboku Oko*). As External Examiner to the Department of Modern European Languages, in the University of Ilorin, he found a particular long essay quite interesting and set it aside to create time to read it over and over, to, as he was to tell me much later, satisfy himself that it was not the product of that ill bedeviling the academic environment, plagiarism. Having thus satisfied himself that it was not plagiarised, he went ahead to score the work an "A".

Finally, to my wife Olubunmi, and children, Barakah, Kareemah, Mubarak and Raheemah, I say thank you to you all for being ever there for Daddy. God bless.

Hakeem Bello

PREFACE

I developed interest in the works of Wole Soyinka quite early. As an undergraduate student at the University of Ilorin between 1984 and 1988, I set time aside for his writings, perusing his plays, novels, poetry, essays, diaries and biographical writings. I felt seriously challenged by most of what I read. For my final year project then, and as part of further tackling the challenges, I decided to study the two novels that he has published till date in an essay titled "Rituals, Violence and Creativity in the Novels of Wole Soyinka." My examiners considered the work outstanding as an undergraduate project and this encouraged me even more in my determination to explore Soyinka further. I therefore decided to return to the subject while pursuing a Masters degree at the University of Ibadan from 1989 through 1991. This time, I elected to study Soyinka's dramatic works for the Masters dissertation I submitted to the University at the end of the programme. The ensuing work was titled "Ritual as Form in Wole Soyinka's Dramaturgy." I had a plan to continue my research on the works of the only Nobel laureate Nigeria has so far produced but my incursion into journalism soon after completing the Masters degree diverted my attention. Since then, all my efforts to return to what should represent my area of primary interest have proved unsuccessful. Recently however, I decided to utilize my rare free moments to take down the two projects and take a fresh look at them. It was then that it re-occurred to me that I had a thread running through both of them. There and then, I made up my mind to create more time to articulate this properly and push it out to a wider readership.

The Interpreters: Ritual, Violence and Social Regeneration is then a re-worked version jointly of my B.A project of 1988 and M.A dissertation of 1990. The uniting thread in the two works is located in the perspective of social regeneration which they explore in the writings of Wole Soyinka. Clearly, Soyinka's concern for a socially reconstructed Nigerian – nay African society – cannot be gainsaid. It stands as the factor that animates his life-long involvement in social and political activism, an involvement which led to his incarceration for two years during the civil war, and his having to flee into exile during the period of Sani Abacha's dictatorship. Soyinka expresses this same concern for social regeneration in his writings, using different metaphors.

The focus of this work lies in the exploration of the articulations of social regeneration specifically in the dramatic and novelistic writings of Wole Soyinka. "The Interpreters" representing the main title of the book has been adopted clearly from the title of Soyinka's first novel and is employed here to refer to a number of characters in Soyinka's different writings who stand as agents of social regeneration. They may suffer for their convictions or even willingly or unwillingly transform to scapegoats in the process of the rites of regeneration. What unites them however, lies in the fact of their being darers of transition, if only to paraphrase Soyinka, standing mid-way in the abyss, receiving visions of social transformation and translating same to their different communities. Eman in *The Strong Breed*, Olunde in *Death and the King's Horseman*, Old Man in *Madmen and Specialists*, Daodu in *Kongi's Harvest*, Isola in *Camwood on the Leaves*, Sekoni in *The Interpreters* and Demakin in *Season of Anomy*, all represent examples of those who qualify to be described as "interpreters" in the context of this book.

The Interpreters: Ritual, Violence and Social Regeneration is divided into two parts. The first part focuses on the dramatic works, and my argument here is that the metaphor adopted by Africa's foremost playwright in articulating his vision of social regeneration is that of ritual. As Soyinka seems to argue in his plays, a society that has lost its moorings needs to undergo rites of expiation and purgation in order to regain direction. For this to be possible, there must emerge a protagonist hero who will possess sufficient qualities of hubris as to make him lead in an act of confrontation with the abyss of transition. The underlying principle is carefully laid out in chapter one and applied in a reading of a selection of plays in chapters two, three, four and five.

The focus of part two is on the novels. Here the metaphor adopted in analyzing the works of Soyinka as a socially committed artist is that of "anjonu". The metaphor has its roots in Yoruba metaphysics and is employed to describe a creature with contradictory personality, one which is committed to the regeneration of the social order while at the same time retaining a vindictive, vengeful nature. The dialectics inherent in the metaphor of "anjonu" is important for understanding Soyinka the novelist. This is because in his novelistic writings, his articulations seem to be to the effect that for the society to be cleansed, those who have corrupted it in the first instance ought to be purged. In other words, and as Soyinka seems to have argued, violence represents an important aspect of the process of social regeneration. Chapter six opens with a brief exploration of this principle before proceeding in the second half to an analysis of *The Interpreters*, Soyinka's first novel. Chapter seven focuses essentially on *Season of Anomy* while chapter eight undertakes a study of the dividing line between ideology and social commitment in the novels of Wole Soyinka. Chapter nine, being the last one, represents simply a brief conclusion to the whole book.

Soyinka is a much studied writer, I need to admit it. Not many of the other writings on him have however brought his drama and novels together in one single study. Even in spite of accomplishing this, *The Interpreters* still stands as a modest effort. I however offer it as my own humble toast to Wole Soyinka as he joins the club of octogenarians.

CONTENTS

❧

PART ONE

THE DRAMAS

Chapter

THE RITUAL IMPERATIVE
IN AFRICAN DRAMA

To attempt to unpack the meaning of the word "ritual" is to consciously submit oneself to the acceptance of the superficiality which modern usage has foisted on the word. Thus, the most attractive option is an explication of the actions from which "ritual" emanates and an attempt to conceptualize or accept existing frameworks for its essence. This way, we would also have succeeded in outlining the principal antecedents of African drama.

Existing postulations on the African metaphysical worldview in the literature foregrounds a hierarchical structure which places an omniscient creator at the helm of affairs over an unspecified number of anthropomorphic beings believed to be similar divinities who must be perennially appeased through rites and sacrifices in order to maintain their favourable disposition. Phenomenal elements are also imbued with life-influencing supernatural powers just as there is a rooted belief in a corresponding ancestral system constantly in communion with the living. Tying all these up, and providing justification for religious practices and its accompanying ritual intricacies is the belief in a spiritual pre-destination which is capable of reparation through the ritual medium.

According to Bolaji Idowu, the above provides the essential outlines in the Yoruba traditional metaphysical world which can also be said to be approximately representative of the African traditional worldview (*Olodumare,* 22). From the above, five belief elements can be identified as forming in combination the structure of African religious system which the traditional man fervently holds dear before the contact with the West and its subsequent impact. These are the beliefs in God, irrespective of local and regional colorations as to his nature, location, sex and manifestations; the divinities; spirits; ancestors; and lastly, the practice of magic and medicine.

The elements of religion established above emanate not out of mundane human interactions but out of man's desperate search for sanity and security in the tempo-spatial landscape which he inhabits, the earth, that is. Four main factors could be outlined as being responsible for this state of desperation according to Joe de Graft (1976:3-4). First, is the awareness of the danger posed by the exterior environment which is charged with such elemental phenomena as lightning, darkness, flood, holocausts, drought, earthquake and other sundry natural disasters. Secondly, there is a yearning for balance in the biochemical processes as a prerequisite for well-being which could be upset not only by hunger, thirst, and suffocation but, and this may seem contradictory, other essential means of sustenance in liquid form like water. Again, fellow creatures both beasts and men are capable of inflicting injury on man as a result of ill will, hatred, envy and evil eye. Beasts and men encompass the myriad spirits and apparitional entities who inhabit phenomena like rocks, mountains, hills, forests and so on. Idowu has described a number of ways in which they are conceived. He asserts: "they may be anthropomorphically conceived, but they are more often than not thought of as powers which are almost abstract, as shades or vapours which take on human shape, they are immaterial and incorporeal beings" (*African Traditional Religion,* 86). Lastly, man is plagued by threats from forces buried within his own soul like pride, anger, covetousness, lust, greed, jealousy and most important of all, fear.

Man's confrontation with all the above leads to religious practices the components of which we have already examined. J.C. de Graft puts the outcome of the threats to man's existence thus:

> It was the awareness of the many threats that led "primitive" man to those rituals of apprehension, propitiation, purification of which impersonation was of such a cardinal feature (1976:3).

These rituals involve sacrifices, but the materials employed for it, the degree of its elaborateness and human participation are determined by the magnitude of the occasion which warrants it in the first place. Thus, ritual celebrations could involve the entire community if its fate is at stake or it could entail mere rites performed within the enclosure of the household shrines. Femi Osofisan, citing the authority of Germaine Dieterlen, has identified five primary occasions when such rituals are performed. These are during collective ceremonies such as those marking seasonal transitions, rites of passage in human life (birth, circumcision, initiation, marriage, death, etc); graduation ceremonies in artisanal vocations (such as smithery, carpentry, leather works); state occasions (such as royal enthronement or priestly appointment); and lastly periods of unusual "mishap" (such as malady, pestilence, migration or war) (1978:42).

In fact, such rituals punctuate every point of human existence and even beyond as could be seen in the communion between man and divinities, as well as between man and ancestors during festivals earmarked for them as noted earlier on. What remains unsaid between Osofisan and Dieterlen is that the intensity of such rituals also depends on the status of its protagonists and spiritual significance. For example, most sacred communal rituals are those involving transitions in the royalty and other related personages.

However, a more fundamental question at this juncture has to do with whether rituals per se can be considered as drama; or whether there is any established connection between celebrations of transitions – a birth or a death, the ritual evocation or incarnation of a god, or ancestor – and drama or theatre? Drama draws its materials from everyday life and the complexities involved in human existence itself could be regarded as drama. However, drama is not and cannot be placed on the same plane as everyday life just as no representation in auditory form like songs and dialogue or visual medium like painting could take the place of an actual activity like farming.

Within this perspective, we could examine two existing scholarly definitions of drama against the background of a cultural setting in the universal sense. Lisbeth Gant says, it is " 'an imitation of an action ... or of a person or persons in action' the ultimate object of which is to edify or to entertain." While according to de Graft (1976:3) "Drama is a condensation from everyday life, whose many aspects – visible and invisible, tangible and intangible – it attempts to manifest, embody or affirm." Thus, drama can be described as a unique art form because apart from drawing its subject from human life it also utilizes actual human bodies, attributes and behaviour as an intrinsic medium of expression. However, drama's ultimate relationship with life manifests clearly when elements of impersonation or role playing are employed in normal existence as a means of achieving certain set goals.

This then pinpoints rituals as the source of drama, for an integral aspect of rituals as seen earlier on, is impersonation.

Taken at the surface level, its purpose could be taken to be merely to entertain but at a deeper psychological level it becomes an attempt to empathize physically, emotionally and intellectually with forces which threaten man's existence. Again, we find the summation of de Graft apt when he describes drama as a perennial search whose essence is predetermined:

> A reaching out by the whole man toward sanity through vicarious experience, whether as an impersonator who himself assumes the identity of the inimical forces or their more powerful opposites, or as a celebrant who seeks identification with an impersonator acting as mediator between him and the forces concerned. In either case, the call is on our powers of empathy, those powers through which human beings are able to enter into the experience of people and objects and so reach an understanding of, or come to terms with, life and the world around them (1976:5).

Thus far, we have established the motif for the ritual celebration and already implied that its important elements include the presence of priests or officiating ministers in the process, the persona or persons in the ritual arena such as scapegoat, or vehicle of empathy as well as members of the community who constitute the audience and participants. The decision to enter a state of impersonation is a conscious one. However, it requires both physical and psychological preparation. The impersonator therefore is helped into a state of readiness through music, choreographed dancing, incantations and spells all of which form dramatic ritual components.

Yet, there are other aspects of enactments which do not fall within the realm of ritual, though they also represent imitations or recreation of an experience or forces. Hence, scholars of African drama like Clark (1981:57-74) and Rotimi (1981:77-80) often try to construct lines of demarcation between ritual drama and secular and pure entertainment within ritual festivals. Of the examples that abound in the literature of such festivals; we take three representative ones to illustrate our position. They should also help us establish other particularities of drama present in the ritual celebration.

The oft-quoted precursor of European drama, the Greek theatre, is universally agreed to have developed from Dionysian festivals. To leave that apart, even within the Western landscape, what can be regarded as the first manifestations of drama emerged within a religious context. This was in the cultural renaissance of the Middle Ages where a short Easter play, called the *Quem quaeritis* dialogue re-enacts the Christian belief of life over death through the resurrection of Jesus Christ. Its dramatic components entail four lines of dialogue initiated by a couple of priests arranged as angels who come out to announce Christ's resurrection to two other priests costumed as women (*Cassell's Encyclopedia I* : 216).

In the local context, correlations of this on a more elaborate scale could be found in the Obatala festival celebrated annually in Osogbo, Western Nigeria. The event it enacts is usually described as the ritual imprisonment of Obatala whose virtues have been agreeably described by J.P. Clark (1981:59) as being "not unlike those of the crucified Christ". The events of the second day of the festival are particularly relevant for it features activities which bring us close to the domain of the passion play, utilizing mime, music, dance, procession to re-enact the earthly life of Obatala. The dramatic story is supplied by the mock duel between Ajagemo (the Chief Priest) and a lower chief Olunwi in which the former is taken prisoner and whisked off from the palace to be released only after the intervention of the Oba who pays a ransom to Olunwi. Ajagemo then returns to the palace amidst a triumphal procession. Ulli Beier succinctly brings out the mimetic empathic significance of this dramatic enactment thus:

> The dancing of this simple (story) as performed at Ede takes only a few minutes, but it is immensely moving largely because of the qualities put into this part by the Ajagemo. There is no question of mere acting. The ability to suffer and not to retaliate is one of the virtues every Obatala worshipper must strive to possess (1969:14).

Lastly, we briefly examine aspects of mimesis emanating from the religious worship of the Kalabaris complex belief system as recorded by Robin Horton (1981:81-112). The Kalabaris divide their universe into spheres of existence: the "Oju" or material and the "teme" the spiritual or immaterial. To cope with their numerous gods, the spiritual world is divided into two separate systems of gods who merit recognitions and worship. The first, called arbiters of form and process – "Tamuno "and "So" are withdrawn. A restricted contact is maintained through periodic invocation and offerings the results of which people await. However, the second is made up of the village Heroes, the water people and the ancestors are more approachable and maintain a closer interaction with the people. Each possesses differing mythological origin and performs specific functions within the Kalabari world, though they invariably complement each other. Due to their nature, "the approach to them becomes a more elaborate affair, altogether richer in the sentiments it draws upon" (Horton: 59).

Preparations for the "approach" commence with the praise chants by a chorus of women singers highlighting their characters and notable achievements. This is followed by details of communal offerings and invocations. However the high point of the religious festival is the human dramatization of the presence of the "gods as guests" at the occasion through set behaviours eliciting responses of dramatic intensity performed by the people to the invited gods. Three modes of dramatic rituals are used to accomplish this: mime, masquerade and possession.

In miming, members of the "Ekine" (communal cult of adults) impose a curfew in the evening and through nasal manipulations reproduce the "voice" of the dead demanding food and drinks from women and housewives in the village. The element of mimesis and make-belief necessary for the drama has been summed up by Horton:

> In all this the victims of the mime are as much in on its secret as are the performers. No woman and few children of talking age are under any illusion that their callers are

other than human – nor are they supposed to be. Yet when they are ordered to get off their mats and bring out food, they do so with an acquiescence which they never show on other occasions ... (1981: 90).

Similar responses are elicited through various ritual particulars in Masquerades to represent the village heroes, water people and the dead. In possession, a god is induced to take over the spirit of a man's body for the same set of gods through elaborate costuming and cultic ritual practices on the chosen. The event is characterized by dance, singing, drumming and role-playing, thus, fulfilling all the preconditions for drama except that straight-forward acting and the formal distance between the stage and the audience are absent.

However, we must hasten to point out that not all rituals involving costumes, dancing, singing and impersonation are drama. Hence, the Gelede masquerade of Egbado, Ketu and the Eyo festival of Lagos cannot be regarded as drama since no mimesis is involved in both. The former takes place in the form of displays to appease witches in the society while the latter is used to represent the spirit of dead ancestors.

Having gone thus far in elucidating the emergence and manifestations of drama in African ritual practices, it is safe to return to our earlier task of establishing a framework within which ritual can be perceived or defined. The separate summations of de Graft and Lisbeth Gant on the nature and place of "ritual" in drama become prerequisites for the evolvement of drama all of which hang on the presence of "ritual". We cite three of them:

1. a world-view which predisposes the people to ritual practice requiring a strong element of role-playing;
2. an inclination to narrative expression, based on that community's own history and legends, myth and folklore;
3. a strong feeling of social solidarity which, with the emergence of an embryonic form of drama from interaction of conditions 1 and 2 above, fosters the

resultant art form not only as an expression of the community's ethos but, perhaps more important, as a means of further strengthening its sense of cohesion and identity (1976:11).

From the above, we have been put on the path of the process to transposing ritual as a communal practice of worship to its evolution into a viable form with very valuable formal and thematic potentials in the theatre. Lisbeth Gant's definition of the phenomenon of "ritual" provides a framework for the content and format of the completely transposed ritual concept. We are compelled by the import of his postulations to quote him at length on the component of ritual:

> First, the emphasis is on the idea that there is a "story" to tell ... The question is not supposed to be, will people respond, but how. And ideally it should be a flowing, spiritual one that allows them to feel a bond of some kind. Second, there is always supposed to be a dual participation ... The spectators are definitely supposed to take part in the ritual. . . Third, there must be a message. The art is used to set people thinking in a certain way for a certain goal. Fourth, usually certain phrases or words come up again and setting up some sort of rhythmic pattern. This may vary from a complete chant to a chorus ... built upon and reinforced to a crescendo and finale. Fifth, the music. Invariably there is not just the rhythm but music as well, which aids in setting up the rhythm and sustaining it (1972: 51).

The above, apart from providing perceptive insight, into the concept of ritual as will be studied in the work, appears like a researched summary of the ritual dramaturgy of the playwright under study. Next, we turn our attention to Soyinka's interpretation of the African metaphysical worldview through which he has established the theory of ritual drama and also the essential components of the dramaturgy resulting from this theory.

Wole Soyinka's Philosophical Constructs for the Theory of Ritual Drama

Soyinka's manifesto as a creative artist is spelled out in earnest declaration: "I cannot claim a transparency of communication even from the sculpture, music and poetry of my own creative inspiration" (1988:329). Thus, the profitable take-off point for a study of Soyinka's aesthetic vision is his distillation of the Yoruba cosmology into a vibrant literary theory from which emerges the theory of ritual drama and the sundry components that constitute the ritual dramaturgy. The thesis of this literary theory is his view centring on the continued location of the quest for communal harmony within the premise of African traditional legacies, the source components of this legacy being the past, to be reached through history, myth and ritual. The call for a non-narcissistic recourse to the past is emphatically stressed in the declaration:

> that wrench within the human psyche which we vaguely define as "tragedy" is the most insistent voice that bids us return to our sources. There illusively hovers the key to the human paradox, to man's experience of being and non-being, his dubiousness as essence and matter (*Myth, Literature,* 140).

However, conscious of the anti-Negritude stance of the writer, it is important to stress at once that the call for a return to the past is from a functional perspective and not for elitist adornment as practiced by the group he criticized. The statement is totally in line with Soyinka's long held notion of the past which made him assert once that:

> Of course, the past exists, the real African consciousness establishes this ... the past exists now, this moment, it is co-existent the present awareness. It clarifies the present and explains the future, but it is not a flesh pot for escapist indulgence, and it is vitally dependent on the sensibility that recalls it (1988:80).

Thus, if the recource to the past is inspired by a yearning for group survival and continuity, its manifestation could be located in the perennial rapport craved often by the human community with the personages, phenomenal elements and other forces mentioned earlier on. This need, posits de Graft, "inspired the naturalistic and embryonic drama in African societies (and) bound humanity together: those gone before, those here now and those to come – with the animate world of rock, fire, wind, water, plant, animals, demon and God!" (1976:13). These rituals we assert earlier on correspond with the community's fabrics of life, fears, hope and aspirations.

Correlates of de Graft's postulations are intrinsically identifiable in Soyinka's dramatic pre-occupation with the ritual arena. The theoretical groundwork for these views has been articulated in his various essays such as "The Fourth Stage" reworked in *Myth, Literature and the African World*, and "Drama and the Idioms of Liberation" all written at different periods but now collected together in *Art, Dialogue and Outrage* edited by Biodun Jeyifo .

We embark henceforth on the explication of these views as an important prerequisite for the thesis of our study. Again, it will help shift attention from the general speculations of de Graft to the concrete particularities of an environment we are familiar with, the Yoruba milieu. According to Soyinka (1971:87), Yoruba metaphysics hold(s) the view of there being three areas of existence – the world of the unborn, the world of the dead, and the world of the living ... (and that) there is a mutual correspondence between these three areas. He goes further to declare his belief in

> a fourth stage which is not often articulated but which I recognize as implicit. It is obviously made concrete by rituals, by the philosophy that is articulated by the Ifa priests. This is the fourth stage – the area of transition. It is the chthonic realm, the area of really dark spirits, the really dark forces and it is also the area of stress of human will (87).

In addition to the personages of this cyclical continuum, the community also invests phenomenal elements already discussed with power. The efficacy of these forces of nature can be seen in the various Yoruba incantations evoking their power. We cite an example of one documented in Duro Ladipo's *Oba Ko So*. Timi, one of Sango's war lords, in venturing into unfamiliar enemy territory, appeals for support from the enabling potency of phenomenal elements. Timi chants:

> It is the gentle wind that says, blow towards me,
> spirits of swarming termites, I say swarm me today.
> Two hundred lizards support the wall
> Let all hands be raised to sustain me.
> (*Three Yoruba Plays*: 30)

The psychic consciousness of these phenomenal forces and the consolidated attempts at grappling with them by man constitute a major pre-occupation of Soyinka's ritual drama as our textual explications will later reveal. However, inseparably connected with the above is Soyinka's perception and interpretation of man's links with the divinities in the Yoruba cosmos. Going by the Yoruba myth of creation, the cosmic landscape originally encompassed man and divinity in a unified essence – the divine oneness of the God-Head. This God-Head was alone, attended by a slave, Atunda. The slave for unrevealed reasons one day rolled a huge boulder on, and shattered, the original essence while tending a farm below a hill. This act of apostasy liberated the divine and human essence hitherto housed in one being. The point of the myth is that both humanity and divinity emanating from a common being shared a certain essence between them which necessitates a groping towards each other. A kind of all-encapsulating empathic imperative is the nature of this essence.

The gods by virtue of their hierarchy first felt the pain and collectively initiated an itinerary whose terminal point is the abode of man in a bid for a re-unification with man – the separated essence. The consequent invasion of the earth and the metaphysical intricacies involved which we shall soon come to elucidate constitute the first tragic rite of passage, thus subsequently becoming the paradigm of African tragic art. A more apparent testimony to this primal interaction in the cosmos is observable in the deification and syncretism seen in the Sango saga and again through the ritual placation of the unborn who are accorded the dignity deemed befitting any member of the feared nether world.

Three hero-gods in the forefront of the primal tragic rite of passage namely, Ogun, Sango, and Obatala are employed by Soyinka to explicate the various complex cosmic interactions during the journey. When examined bearing in mind the antagonizing world of Esu, the ubiquitous god of chance, against whom these gods have to contend in Soyinka's drama, their destinies become paradigmatic. Their myriad cosmic interactions contain portents implicating man, animal, phenomenal elements and the divinities themselves. The principal protagonist of this primal tragic rite was Ogun, going by the myth. He is also the central persona in Soyinka's ritual drama and hence will constitute the focus of our analytical attention. However, because of their relevance both to this work and Soyinka's dramaturgy, we examine several general issues relating to the other gods since we will have to make references to them later.

Inherent in the nature of all the divinities are human attributes including virtues and foibles. In fact, the only edge they maintain over humanity is the assumed notion of their immortality. Thus, like humanity, the dual creative-destructive essence is an inherent component in the make-up of the divinities. The awareness of these facts is expressed by Soyinka thus:

> Common to all these gods, it may be remarked at this point, is that even when, like Obatala, they bear the essence of purity, their history is always marked by some act of excess, hubris or other human weakness. The consequences are significantly, measured in human terms and such gods are placed under an eternal obligation of some practical penance which compensates humanity (1976:13).

It is clear from the above statement that the weakness need not emanate from negative acts. Excessive passivity just like excessive anger, strength or weakness could upset balance in the cosmic psyche. The emerging implication is that, just like that of man, the actions of the divinities could now and again activate a disruption in the communal psyche. Thus, in spite of Obatala's exclusive preserve for drink, this grave weakness poses a danger to his office, for he is the god of "plastic creativity" charged with the moulding of human forms. Once getting tipsy on palmwine, he fumbled and cripples, albinos, the blind and such often malformed creations were churned out in numbers. A disruption in the psyche was thereby perpetrated and had to be atoned for.

Accounts of this atonement have resulted in the creation of a fine play, *The Imprisonment of Obatala,* even cited by Soyinka in his presentation. The original error committed by Obatala necessitated his rite of passage, a trip during which untold hardship, and privations became his lot. The climax of this suffering is his imprisonment in the hands of Sango whose action stems from Esu's machinations. This would not have been so, had he revealed his identity but this would have breached the process of penance, hence contradicting his attributes – humility and passivity through which he has been divined to prosper *(The Imprisonment:* 33). However, his imprisonment engenders a dislocation in the communal psyche and more painfully so, the human world. The god ceased to function in prison and his duties of eliciting rain and turning blood into children was halted. This resulted in chaos, confusion and afflictions. This is seen in the following lines from Ijimere's play:

> A curse has fallen on Oyo
> The corn on its stalk is worm eaten
> And hollow like an old honeycomb;
> The yam in the earth is dry and stringy like palm fibre ...
> Creation comes to a standstill
> When he who turns blood into children
> Is lingering in jail. *(The Imprisonment:* 31)

Sango's unwitting contribution to the disruption needs to be noted for he became the medium of Obatala's penance. On the face of it, he could not be adjudged guilty of unwarranted imprisonment since he acted on Esu's wily machinations. Yet, he could also not be let off the hook just like that. Thus, he was to discover later that the doom that befell his earthly domain was entirely of his own making. The lesson to be drawn from the myth is that the mishap could have been averted if Sango had been less hubristic to heed both Babalorisa (the diviner) and Oya's admonitions to him with regards to the identity of his captive. Thus, the proud god of "retributive justice" became humiliated ultimately on discovering his responsibility for the gross injustice done to Obatala, and the untold hardship foisted on the subjects whom he was supposed to be protecting. In applying the paradigm outlined above to the ritual drama of the playwright, it is essential to note the destiny of the gods, their dual god-man attributes, their weaknesses precipitating communal psychic dislocations and the subsequent precipitation of acts of penance for the restoration of cosmic harmony. Again, notice must be taken of Soyinka's assertion to the effect that:

> "Morality for the Yoruba is that which creates harmony in the cosmos" (1976:156).

Inherent in the two conclusions are the essential thematic ingredients of ritual dramaturgy which are presented in varying proportions in Soyinka's theatre. In other words, the responsibility for the maintenance of order, harmony and continuity is shared between the gods and humanity in the African cosmos. The pre-occupation of Soyinka's contemporary theatre and dramaturgy is the celebration of the various ways in which disruption occurs in the communal psyche and the attempts to achieve the cosmic restoration of continuity and order. The paradoxical link between death as a prerequisite for the discovery of the meaning of life becomes very important here. This complementary parity has its origin in the disintegration of the original godhead. As Soyinka tells us, "the fragmentation of the original godhead may be seen, however, as fundamental to man's resolution of the experience of birth, and the disintegration of consciousness in death"

(*Myth, Literature:* 33). Death therefore is the greatest threat to life or continuity. Hence a recurring theme in the ritual theatre of Soyinka is the confrontation with death as a communal attempt to ensure life and maintain continuity.

Secondly, and in the same vein, Soyinka's ritual theatre is also devoted to drawing man's attention to the precipitation of those hubristic acts which could lead to the breakdown of harmony in the society. Both objectives are achieved in the drama of Soyinka employing ritual as theme and technique in a variety of ways. This I shall soon focus on in my discussion of the structure of ritual in the playwright's dramaturgy.

However, there is a need to return directly to a number of postponed issues which have a close connection with our earlier claims. These are the questions of the central dramatis personae in the playwright's ritual drama. Ogun, probably long endeared to Soyinka by his exploits and multi-faceted manifestation is the artist's muse. Again, the totality of his primal tragic experience provides the paradigm on which the tragic protagonist is moulded: "Ogun is the embodiment of challenge, the promethean instinct in man, constantly at the service of society for its full self-realisation."

The history of Ogun is the story of the completion of the Yoruba cosmogony because his rite of passage enabled its coming into being. Ogun was indisputably the first deity to dare the abyss of transition, an account of which has been succinctly rendered by Soyinka thus:

> A long isolation from the world of men had created an impossible barrier which they tried, but failed to demolish. Ogun finally took over. Armed with the first technical instrument which he had forged from the ore of mountain wombs, he cleared the primordial jungle, plunged through the abyss and called on the others to follow (*Myth, Literature:* 29).

For this hubristic act, Ogun faced threats of disintegration from the cosmic winds of the abyss. To contain this threat of dissolution he summoned his enormous will and courage to his assistance.

Implicit here is that Ogun became the first "actor" and through the forging of the "ore of mountain-wombs" his creative essence came to the fore. However, this act of hubris carries with it a penalty. On this, another myth takes charge, but reduced to bare essentials goes thus. The gods, impressed by Ogun's feat offered him a crown for monarchical authority over them which he declined. Human beings were also to tempt him again and again. The gods, having dispersed on arrival on earth, Ogun settled amidst the hospitality of the people of Ire. To recompense his host, Ogun promptly routed their enemies in the next battle. Anxious to retain his superhuman dexterity, Ire people offered Ogun the crown which he eventually accepted after much petition. The humans were ignorant of Ogun's knowledge of the unpredictable resurgence of his violent aspects. This, people were to painfully realize when back at the battle field, Ogun fell for the tricks of Esu, the wily trickster, gulping a keg of palmwine left for him. At the high point of intoxication, friend and foe became game for the warlord, routing them with record rapidity.

In Soyinka's dramaturgic ensemble, the earthly tragic protagonist is imbued with corresponding attributes. Thus, according to Obisesan (1986:136), Soyinka's protagonist simply, "is involved, wittingly or unwittingly in struggles of life and death. Whether on behalf of the community or in his individual capacity, the result is ultimately communal in implication and effect." This is even more so for the tragic works of Soyinka which are in the main "rituals of archetype" involving an aspiring community originally found in "the Fourth Stage" striving to reunite with the other – the ancestors, the dead and the unborn. Such ritual protagonists are either self-chosen like Professor in *The Road,* or communally chosen as in the cases of Demoke in *A Dance of the Forest,* Eman in *The Strong Breed* and Elesin Oba in *Death and the King's Horseman.*

Secondly, from our discourse thus far, it must be clear the prominent role of myth in the realization of Soyinka's ritual objectives. The first drama theorist, Aristotle (1971:48-66) prefers that materials for drama be drawn from myth rather than from the actuality of history – past or contemporary. However, to achieve relevance, contemporary writers like Soyinka cannot afford a narrow pre-occupation with myth alone. Yet myth and ritual cannot be separated from contemporary reality especially in the context of African cosmic perception because "the assimilative wisdom of African metaphysics recognizes no difference in essence" (1976:140). Thus, for Soyinka, myth and ritual become mediating vehicles both for celebrating continuity in human existence and for interpreting contemporary experience of diverse nature. The justification for this resides in Soyinka's assertion that:

> a fortunate blend of myth and history, penetrates even deeper into that area of man's cosmogonic hunger, one which leads him to the profounder forms of art as retrieval vehicles for, or assertive links with, a lost sense of origin (*Myth, Literature*: 54).

Lastly, a major component of the ritual drama hinted on earlier through Lisbeth Gant's framework is language. Ritual language in tragic drama draws from subliminal resources and is often employed in a distinct way to contain the spiritual, emotional and empathic tempo of the tragic landscape. Hence, in the ritual arena "words are taken back to their roots, to their original poetic sources when fusion was total and the movement of words was the passage of music and the dance of image" (*Myth, Literature*: 147).

This is to enhance the tragic passage at the highpoint of the ritual when the living, the dead and the unborn are linked in the gulf of transition. The lyricist at this moment is transformed into the mouthpiece of the chthonic forces rendering hitherto unknown mythopoeic strains already residual in the numinous arena of transition and eliciting a gripping antiphonal refrain from the ritual participant (*Myth, Literarure*: 148). There is a conscious attempt to capture this masonic quality in the ritual drama of Soyinka.

Thus far, we have examined the basic philosophical constructs of Soyinka's theory of ritual drama. We have also explicated the various elements encompassed in the dramaturgy emanating from this theory. However, in both the formulation of this theory and its transposition on stage or in the play-text, Soyinka borrows or draws from existing western dramatic techniques. In fact, his dramatic theories can be described as an original re-interpretation of earlier theories of tragedy especially by Wilson G. Knight and Friedrich Nietzsche both of whom he often acknowledges and refers to. Hence, a proper assessment as well as the discovery of the other potentials of Soyinka's dramatic theory emerges through a critical look at these earlier theories. Secondly, a discernible formal and thematic pattern is identifiable in Soyinka's application of ritual aesthetics in his works which constitute the focus of this study. Thus, we now shift attention to the strains of the western in Soyinka's theory and practice of ritual drama and the structure of ritual in his oeuvre. These will help complete the formulation of the theoretical background for our studies.

Strains of the Western ...

As said earlier on, Soyinka's dramatic theory evolves out of an original reworking of existing Western ritual approaches to drama through the particularities of Yoruba cosmology. Hence, its essence could only be properly appreciated in relation to the extractions, modifications and expressions derived from these previous theories. The origin of the theory which establishes a link between ritual and drama could be traced to Aristotelian postulations on the nature of tragedy. Ritual and drama posits Aristotle (1971:48), emanates from "the authors of the dithyramb." The only other insight provided by the *Poetics* in establishing the link between ritual and drama is Aristotle's definition of tragedy which revolves around the concept of audience affect: "through pity and fear effecting the proper purgation of these emotions" (50).

However, a more profitable starting point for the comparative study of Soyinka's theory is the theories of tragedy formulated by Friedrich Nietzsche and G. Wilson Knight both of whom have speculated extensively on the link between drama and ritual. Nietzsche's theory is essentially based on Greek tragedy. He took off on a note of agreement with Aristotle's premise on the Dionysian dithyramb origin of tragedy. According to him, Apollo, the Greek moral deity demanded self-control from his people. In order to observe such restraint vital for the maintenance of communal harmony (the kind in Yoruba cosmology), a knowledge of self was considered necessary. The imperative for balance here being "nothing too much". Excesses leading to disruption of the balance are viewed as being master-minded by hostile spirits who are outside the sphere of Apollonia, but part of that of Dionysos. But the Greeks were soon to discover that their whole existence maintained by Apollo's temperate beauty, rested upon a base of suffering hidden from them until it was revealed by the reinstatement of the deposed Dionysos. After a long period of discord between them, "the pair accepted the yoke of marriage and in this condition, begot Attic tragedy, which exhibits the salient features of both parents" (1971:636).

However, Nietzsche goes further to posit that in tragedy "ritual dithyramb becomes symbolic of universal and individual conflicts." Thus, the effect of the tragic ritual on the audience is that through the medium of drama the individual gains what Ann Davis (1972:148) citing the authority of Micheal Hinden describes as the "subliminal perception of a communal consciousness." This perception is achieved at the point when members of the audience become aware of the correlates between the dramatic conflict and his internal psychological conflict both as an individual and as a member of a social group. A replica of this conflict of the individual could be found within the "world will" between the principles of fusion and individuation. Correlates of this stance could also be found in Aristotle's concept of learning through the drama of limitation. He asserts that: "the reason why men enjoy seeing a likeness is that in contemplating it, they find themselves learning or inferring and saying perhaps, 'Ah that is he' (49). Again it could also be found in Soyinka's stance of the regenerative effects of the tragic conflict of Ogun on the individual.

Wilson Knight (1962), being more of a contemporary critic, while accepting Nietzsche's deduction on the metaphorical link between the experience of ritual and that of tragic drama, extends this relationship beyond Greek ritual and drama to incorporate later postulations from the Elizabethan age through to the neo-classics and down to modern drama. Knight focuses like other modern theorists on wider areas of psychological conflict than that emphasized by Nietzsche. The premise of Knight in discussing ritual in psychoanalytical terms concentrates on psycho-sexual conflicts. He asserts that: "Ritual and drama are agents; as civilization advances the agency become more psychological but its action persists" (8).

While agreeing with Nietzsche and Knight on the metaphorical link between the experience of ritual and that of drama, Soyinka's theory departs radically from those of the two in a number of ways. First, Soyinka formulated a theory based on contemporary drama as contrasted with Nietzsche's pre-occupation with Greek drama and Knight's review of same. Secondly, the theory focuses on social and psychological processes rather than the individual alone. Thirdly, Soyinka widened the scope of ritual and dramatic potentials. Thus, according to Ann Davis, "Soyinka is equally concerned with defining the experience of drama in relationship to revolutionary, or liberating, social consciousness" (148).

Thus, by this all -embracing response inspired in each individual, a collective awareness of cultural values and mythic impulses of the community is engendered. The existence of a relationship between ritual and revolutionary consciousness in the dramatic theory of Soyinka opens up a fresh insight into my analysis which will continue to unfold as I go on. For now it is sufficient to stress that Soyinka's concept of ritual drama unfolds from a broad perspective. This is obvious from the various definitions he provides in the essay "Drama and the Revolutionary ideal" where he categorically declares that "ritual is the language of the masses" and also describes ritual as a "universal idiom" (1975:61-88).

Furthermore, in reaction to the seemingly endless foisting of the often misconceived tag of tragic pessimism as his sole aesthetic vision, Soyinka has outlined the endless possibilities of the ritual drama.

> The truly creative writer who is properly uninhibited by ideological wind — chooses — and of course we can speculate on the sociological factors in this choice ad infinitum – he chooses when to question accepted history as in *A Dance of the Forests;* when to appropriate ritual for ideological statements - The *Bacchae of Euripides* and equally, when to "epochalise" History for its mythopoeic resourcefulness as in *Death and the King's Horseman* (Who's Afraid of Elesin Oba": 126).

The purpose of the above is to serve a note of caution on the aspiring critic to be wary of holistic declarations inspired by an evaluation of a few randomly selected texts. Thus, the keyword to the study of the complex and multi-faceted aesthetic vision of a major playwright like Soyinka is open-mindedness which becomes an enabling concept for a complete and adequate comprehension of the immense dimensions of his work. Our establishment of the structure of rituals in the playwright's drama has been guided by this foresight.

Structure of Rituals in Wole Soyinka's Dramaturgy

Ropo Sekoni (1987) who has expressed reservations on the attitude of critics of ritual in African drama who view ritualistic elements in individual texts as autonomous phenomena rather than as "devices to use existing structures within the lore of the audience's community as metaphor for and comments about contemporary problems and pre-occupations" largely corroborates our conclusions above. Thus, to avoid the pitfall of a strait-jacket approach to the study of ritual as form in Soyinka's dramaturgy, we have tried to evolve a model which at once

encapsulates both the metaphysical, aesthetic and communicative aspects of social behaviour. Hence, we have identified the
following formal and thematic continuum in the ritual drama of
Wole Soyinka.

The primal pre-occupation of Soyinka as shown in our
explications of his dramatic theory is the celebration of the various
ways in which communal dislocations occur in the community
and the various attempts at the cosmic restoration of continuity
and order. Here, death as the dual parity and central companion
as well as threat to life is being confronted by a ritual protagonist
either chosen or self-chosen – as earlier pointed out – on behalf
of the community to ensure continuity and communal regeneration. In such plays, ritual becomes not only form but even subject
matter. The works in this category are *The Strong Breed* and *Death
and the King's Horseman*. Second is the group of plays in which
ritual tragedy forms a framework for the dramatic actions in
alerting society to the threats of the "the returning cycle" of the
potent forces of psychic dislocations, the ultimate aim being to
question acceptable history or values, habits or practices to pave
way to the call for change. Among such plays are *A Dance of the
Forests, Madmen and Specialists* and *The Road*. Thirdly, are plays
in which the ritual medium becomes a communicative tool for
the liberation of either the individual and/or communal social
consciousness. Plays examined under this category are *The
Bacchae of Euripides, Kongi's Harvest, The Swamp Dwellers,
Camwood on the Leaves* and *The Lion and the Jewel*.

Present in all the categories are elements which could bear
description as constants of ritual dramaturgy – the protagonists,
the mediators, the chorus and other participants. Also present
are the indispensable aesthetic components of ritual drama:
mime, music, drumming, dancing and myriad techniques used to
enact the ritual spectacle such as flashbacks, word-play and
distorted festival forms.

Our first three chapters (apart from the introduction) are
devoted to an analysis of the established formal and thematic
continuum. The fourth studies the recurrent elements of ritual

dramaturgy highlighted in the theory as employed in all the plays in varying proportions. Lastly, we attempt a critique of the value, viability, contribution and potentialities of ritual aesthetics in contemporary African drama. With the outlined as my aim, I hope, in the end, to affirm or debunk Ann B. Davis' assertion that Soyinka's theory of dramatic rituals enhances a major development:

> an approach to drama which does not focus exclusively on tragedy, utilizes an inclusive concept of ritual, and treats a broad range of social and psychological processes within the dramatic experience (1972:153).

Chapter

2

❦

RITUAL AS FORM AND MATTER IN THE DRAMA OF COMMUNAL REGENERATION

Transition is the central enabling metaphor of renewal or regeneration. It is one of the occasions which I outlined in Chapter One as engendering communal celebration. I also pointed it out then that the scale and material scope of such a celebration is determined by the magnitude of the occasion which warrants it. Transition manifests either at seasonal juncture – the end of a new year and the beginning of a new one, or as the transmogrification in existence from one realm to the other, involving a principal personage like the king. During such important events, the fate of the state is at stake. Hence, all resources are harnessed towards ensuring an undisrupted transition through an unbroken link between the cyclic continuum – the living, the unborn and the dead – to secure cosmic order.

For, in spite of the existing link between the three worlds, cosmic forces first encountered by the primal tragic hero persistently threaten man with disjunction. The challenges of these cosmic forces must be constantly met as Soyinka asserts:

> Yoruba does not... fail to distinguish between himself and the deities, between himself and the ancestors, between the unborn and his reality, or discard his awareness of the essential gulf that lies between one area of existence and another. The gulf is what must be constantly diminished by the sacrifices, the ritual, the ceremonies of appeasement of those power which lie guardian to the gulf (Myth, Literature: 144).

Despite the guardians of the gulf, a major threat to communal psyche is the burden of guilt and sin accumulated seasonally to the detriment of community's health by members of the community. Thus, ritual sacrifice assumes a dual significance in the human quest for cosmic order through transition: a means of psychological purgation and a bridge in human existence with nature; a design to utilize death to secure future renewal. The ultimate vehicle of transition is the human person, the tragic protagonist acting as the carrier of the community's iniquities or confronting death to ensure communal well-being through the individual will. According to Soyinka, "the whirlpool of transition requires both hubristic complements as catalyst to its continuous regeneration ... All acts are subordinate to these ultimate of the human condition and retroactive will. To dare transition is the ultimate test of human spirit" (Myth, Literature: 58).

To peep outside Soyinka's world of African metaphysics, the concept of scapegoatism itself is a universal phenomenon. Viewed from the perspectives of either psychology or anthropology, it is the act of heaping the community's action, inactions, sins, weaknesses and troubles on a symbolic figure. This practice of symbolic expurgation is as old as human history but originally traceable to the process of atonement in Leviticus whereby Aaron commits the iniquities and transgression of the people of Israel on a goat later driven into the wilderness. The hope then is that "the goat shall bear all their iniquities upon him to a solitary land; and he shall let the goat go in the wilderness" (Leviticus chapter 16: vs 20-28).

The "escape" of the goat into the wilderness is symbolic of a peace pact with God after the confession of sins. Scapegoatism as an act essentially is an appeasement to a deity, a god or a cosmic force to either remove or prevent an evil that may befall a community. Frazer, after an in depth study of the phenomenon among different cultures, has defined it as "the accumulated misfortunes and sins of the whole people ... sometime, laid upon the god, who is supposed to bear them away forever, leaving the people innocent and happy" (*The Golden Bough* Vol. IV: 1).

This directly recalls the picture of Ezeulu transformed into a spirit, and astutely carrying away the woes and travails of Achebe's Igbo community in *Arrow of God*. However, the complexities entailed in the process of communal sacrifice for regeneration transcend the all too simple definition of Frazer. For death is not an ordinary event especially when connected with the fate of the whole community. It involves the moral will of both "the strong breed", the protagonist of the ritual archetype and the community itself whose moral and spiritual preparedness ought to justify the death.

Hence, Soyinka's treatment of the issues of ritual sacrifice and heroism for communal well being both in his theoretical constructs examined earlier on, and the two plays, *The Strong Breed* and *Death and the King's Horseman* assume multifarious dimensions dramatically and thematically as our explications will show. Soyinka believes that society must act in harmony with nature, and that the highest order of morality is that which guarantees the continuity of the species. Thus, for him, the hope is for communal regeneration after a meaningful sacrifice. But when the sacrifice fails to restore harmony in the community the relationship of men to the ancestors, the gods and the unborn remains dislocated even if the sacrifice is the life of a member of the community. However, when the community proves fit morally and spiritually to the sacrifices of the individual, balance is restored and there is an immense possibility of cosmic peace. Herein lies the realm of tragic drama and the major distinction of the artistic vision that emerges at the end of *Death and the King's Horseman* as opposed to that of *The Strong Breed*. The concerns of both plays also go beyond Femi Ososfisan's assertion to the effect that

> the playwright's almost obsessive inquiry into the essence and the apparatus of the society's self-rejuvenating process. Behind this quest is the belief, shared with the traditional artist, that society seasonally accumulates a burden of guilt and sin dangerous to its health and sanity, and which can be purged only through the shedding of human blood ("Tiger On Stage": 163).

More accurately, both plays question the moral justification of Eldred Jone's belief to the effect that Soyinka:

> sees society as being in continual need of salvation from itself. The act of salvation is not a mass act, it comes about through the vision and dedication of individuals who doggedly pursue their vision in spite of the opposition of the society they seek to save. They frequently end up as the victims of the society which benefits from their vision. The salvation of the society then depends on the exercise of the individual will (*Writing of Wole Soyinka:* 11).

The above concern informs our analyses of both plays. However, our critical attention is on laying open Soyinka's manner of employment of ritual as metaphysical, communicational and aesthetic strategies in the works.

The theme of sacrifice as ritual expiation and heroism is developed in *The Strong Breed*. The tradition of a carrier of the sins of the community described by Eman's father is a manifestation of an actual purification ritual among the Igbo people of Nigeria:

> The New Yam festival of the Eastern Region is unique. The people make a miniature canoe and the evil of the town is "spoken" into it. The man who is selected to carry the canoe goes into a trance, amidst drumming and a hypnotic atmosphere. At the signal he lifts the miniature canoe on his head and is chased into the sea. This is followed by sacrifices to welcome the new tide. The Old tide carried the evils away. Everyone who participates in the ritualistic chase bathes in the river: the old year is thus washed away (Adelugba: 1964: 15).

In transferring this ritual prototype into drama, Soyinka employs an unnamed African setting peopled with Eman – the Ogun, Obatala and Christ-like character – the mediators of the ritual (Jaguna and Oroge), the participants or chorus, to achieve maximum effects and make his statements. Eman the tragic hero is seen to challenge, through an act of his will, the laws of man and even the cosmic forces. The action causes an imbalance in the community and the cosmos. The tragic hero must be punished for this daring act which precipitates the disruption. Though his affront is ultimately beneficial, his suffering is a necessary price he must pay for the eventual growth in his own self-awareness and also that of the community and the cosmos.

Eman plays the enlightened teacher and healer in the village where he has only an alien status. He interferes with its ritual affairs thus bringing himself into conflict with the mediators of the transition ritual, that is Jaguna and Oroge who make him a scapegoat. The village is traditionally hostile to strangers. This is seen in Sunma's anxiety to get Eman to leave the village, and in other travellers hurrying to flee the village on the eve of its final transition rituals. The fate of Eman as a stranger becomes inevitable when he harbours the rootless idiot Ifada whom the mediators and his attendants have chosen as a carrier. Thus, Eman's act of hubris in sheltering Ifada shows his contempt for a people whose practices lack the required moral force. This attitude gets him into trouble when he confronts Oroge and Jaguna with the contradiction inherent in forcing an unwilling scapegoat to die for them.

> JAGUNA: Take him out. (The man carries out
> Ifada) You see, it is so easy to talk.
> You say there are no men in this
> village because they cannot
> provide a willing carrier. And yet
> I heard Oroge tell you we only
> use strangers. There is only
> one other stranger in the village
> but I have not heard him offer
> himself ... It is so easy to talk
> Is it not? (*Collected Plays* 1:129-130)

Eman like the primal tragic hero takes up the challenge. However, crisis ensues when in his attempt to escape the ritual beating, he re-entered the village, an act of extraordinary pollution meaning that he has to be killed. Oroge spells the penalty of an uncooperating carrier out when he says to Eman, "You ought to know that no carrier may return to the village. If he does, the people will stone him to death" (129). Thus, the stage appears set for Eman to pay the ultimate price of his hubristic act and more importantly to fulfill the end predicted for him earlier on by his father who insists that there is no escape for one with the blood of the carrier flowing in his veins:

> EMAN: I am unfitted for your work father.
> I wish to say no more. But I am
> Totally unfitted for your call . . .
> OLD MAN: I am very sad. You will only go to give
> others what rightly belongs to us.
> You will use your strength among thieves.
> They are thieves because they take
> what is ours, they have no claim of
> blood to it. They will even lack the
> knowledge to use it wisely. Truth

is my companion at this moment my
son. I know everything I say will
surely bring the sadness of truth (134).

The mediators in *The Strong Breed* are responsible for ensuring an undisrupted transition into the new year, hence both relentlessly pursue their victims, first Ifada and later Eman. The anxiety visible in their actions, resulting in their impatience with Eman and Jaguna's harsh treatment of his daughter, Sunma, who is conspicuously opposed to the evil practices of her father's village result in the knowledge of the consequences of a disrupted ritual. Thus, Jaguna betrays his mounting foreboding when he declares with respect to Eman's escape: "We must find him. It is a poor beginning for a year when our own curses remain hovering over our homes because the carrier refused to take them" (132). Most of the use of ritual as a communication strategy in the play comes through flashbacks which are very significant in it. Through one of them, we are able to see the less dangerous sacrificial ceremonies in which the strong breed engage leading to the healing and renewal of their communities without a loss of their lives as contrasted to Jaguna's ultimate death trap for Eman at the climax of the play: (Enter Eman-as carrier-from the same direction as the last two entered. In front of him is a still figure, the old man as he was, carrying the dwarf boat)

> EMAN: (Joyfully): Father. (The figure does not turn
> round).
> EMAN: It is your son, Eman (He moves nearer) Don't
> you want to look at me? It is I, Eman. (He moves
> closer still.)
> OLD MAN: You are coming too close. Don't you know
> what I carry on my head?
> EMAN: But father, I am your son.
> OLD MAN: Then go back. We cannot give the two of us ...
> (144-145).

This flashback helps Eman prepare himself psychologically as the scapegoat in Jaguna's village. Just as an earlier one, this flashback shows the kind of ritual he should have gone through to get him properly prepared for his journey through the gulf. The next one shows Eman encountering the scene of his father's preparation:

> (An old man, short and vigorous looking is seated on a stool. He also is wearing calf-length baggy trousers, white. On his head, a white cap. An attendant is engaged in rubbing his body with oil. Round his eyes, two white rings have already been marked) (132).

Thus, structurally *The Strong Breed* is designed to enhance a fusion of the past and the present. The visualized scapegoat ritual in flashback contrasts with the one presently experienced by Eman which becomes part of the self-discoveries he finds in his self-imposed exile. One of such discoveries is the loss of his wife displayed also through a flashback. However, its climax is the merging of reality and vision at the end of the play Eman finally fulfils his destiny as tragic protagonist expressed symbolically in the image of the effigy hanging from a tree on the way to the river.

The effigy itself is an important aspect of the ritual. According to Oyin Ogunba "the effigy is the symbolic representation of evil in the community and when it is dragged along people are expected to utter curse on it or simply keep quiet" (1972:109). The effigy belongs to a mysterious girl, as Ogunba suggests, who has been tutored to associate the chronic disease ravaging her with it and to believe that she will be cured once the scapegoat is exiled on the eve of the new year. In more ways than one, the effigy is representative of Eman and symbolic of the fate that awaits him. First, the girl associates it with Eman and goes ahead to demand clothing for it from him. Afterwards, she and the idiot Ifada club the effigy making sure they do not break it into pieces. Traditionally the effigy is hung at the stroke of midnight to signify the disappearance of the disease with the old year. Both the beating and ultimate hanging become the fate of Eman in the course of his trial. First is the beating in the passage offstage which the mediators Jaguna and Oroge report:

OROGE: ... He took the beating well enough.
I think he is the kind who would let
himself be beaten from night till dawn and
not utter a sound. He would let himself be
stoned until he dropped dead (132).

Later he is required to die by hanging for turning back to the
village and polluting it with its old sins probably because of his
ill preparedness for the hubristic act he undertakes.

JAGUNA: ... It is no longer enough to drive
him past every house. There is too much
contamination about already ... The year
will demand more from this carrier than we
thought (135).

The death of Eman and the hanging of his symbol, the effigy, is
depicted in the following stage directions.

(There is a sound of twigs breaking,
of a sudden trembling in the branches
Then silence.) (In front of Eman's house.
The effigy is hanging from the sheaves) (145).

Ordinarily the assumption at this stage of the ritual enactments
is that Eman dies, a substitute for the original scapegoat and the
tragic protagonist carrying through the abyss of transition the
inscrutable girl's disease and the travails of the village. However,
examined just a bit further there are problems with the outcome
of the ritual which in itself is a culmination of events that
prompted Soyinka to make his contemporary statements on the
subject.

The moral will of both Eman's and Jaguna's villages can no
longer justify the human sacrifices as a means of ensuring
transition. Several issues of spiritual significance have been
compromised on both sides even by the leaders and mediators
of the ritual. Thus, in the flashback scene on Eman's initiation
rites, several ills are revealed as defiling the spiritual essence of
the seclusion. The tutor is corrupt morally, and overlooks all the
taboos committed by Omae. In Jaguna's village, the situation is

worse. This is because the village lacks the moral will to support its rituals by providing a scapegoat from within. Again, the mediators Oroge and Jaguna are both corrupt, and willingly compromise the broken taboos in the course of the rituals. This is because they no longer staunchly believe in the efficacy of the rituals which are now handled as mere routines. Apart from these, from within the society, people are already beginning to question the appropriateness of the human sacrifice in ushering in a new year as seen in the vehement repulsion of Sunma to the practice.

All these considered, the guilt produced in the community appears predictable. "(Almost at once, the villagers begin to return, subdued and guilty. They walk across the front, skirting the house as widely as they can. No word is exchanged. Jaguna and Oroge eventually appear ....)"

> JAGUNA: ... But did you see them? One and all
>   they looked up at the man and words
>   died in their throats.
> OROGE: It was no common sight.
> JAGUNA: Women could not have behaved
>   so shamefully. One by one they
>   crept off like sick dogs. No one
>   could even raise a curse.
> OROGE: It was not only him they fled.
>   Do you see how unattended we
>   are? (145-146).

Clearly, there is a feeling of guilt, indicating that the practice is no longer totally acceptable. Against this background the conclusions drawn on the play by Ndumbe Eyoh (1987:72) provides an apt summation of our discussions:

> Soyinka questions the validity of traditional
> sacrifice, but this must not be taken to mean
> that he rejects the whole concept. What he
> advocates is sacrifice which stems from a
> strong moral purpose and is intended
> not just to fulfill the need for ceremonies,
> but to provide a motive force.

If the motivation is absent both at the individual and communal levels in *The Strong Breed*, it is the guiding principle of the community in *Death and the King's Horseman*.

There are two major factual antecedents for the play both of which are central to our analysis. We briefly review them. Babayemi, in giving accounts of the "Bere festival in Oyo" as a national event in the Yoruba speaking world, enumerated the characteristics and functions of the Olokunesin. Of the two ritual ceremonies associated with the festival: Pakundinrin and Jelepa, Olokunesin is entirely responsible for the execution of the former by virtue of the traditional significance of his office which Babayemi sums up thus:

> Olokunesin is the keeper of the king's horses. He is in charge of the grass for feeding the royal horses, but more than this, *he is regarded as the closest to the world of nature among the palace officials.* He is therefore the priest that looks after the growth and productivity of the field. Alafin's energy and well being, through his nature's gift and special is annually renewed. Bere (the first fruit of the field) is offered back to Sango in return. Since the revitalizing and replenishing power Olokunesin possesses terminates with the death of an Alaafin, he too must commit suicide (Emphasis mine) (1973:12).

The importance of the Olokunesin's office as well as the risks it carries marks him out for special treatment. He enjoys limitless privileges which atimes could border on the vindictive and erratic use of his immense powers.

The above background provides an insight into the spiritual implication of a historical event which took place in Oyo in 1946 and which has produced a major play, Duro Ladipo's *Oba Waja*. The major points of the incident as recorded in the play runs thus. That year, as the commander of the Horse, Olokunesin goes through the ritual preparations to will the seizure of his existence so as to join the dead Alaafin of Oyo, the English District Officer in the area at the insistence of his frightened wife, arrests the man and places him in protective custody. Confusion breaks loose, for the spell of ritual has been broken and cosmic disaster threaten the people. Olokunesin's son returns from the Gold Coast where he trades to perform his father's funeral only to encounter his father still alive, terrified and half-relieved by his escape. He sat among his people who hurl insults at him. Driven by a deep sense of shame and fear of the wrath of the gods his son commits suicide. The central theme of this Duro Ladipo play is the disintegration and confusion let upon the people by the white man's interference with tradition.

Thus between the two sources: The Bere festival and the historical incident documented by Duro Ladipo can be found Soyinka's inspiration for *Death and the King's Horseman*. However, we must point out from the outset Soyinka's original handling of the historicity of the pure festival or the historicity of Ladipo's play and this he stresses in his preliminary notes:

> The confrontation in the play is largely metaphysical, contained in the human vehicle which is Elesin and the universe of the Yoruba mind – the world of the living, the dead and the unborn, and the numinous passage which links all: transition (*Six Plays:* 145).

Thus, the ritual subject matter could only be dramatized through a corresponding ritual technique. Says Soyinka, "*Death and the King's Horseman* can be fully realized only through an evocation of music from the abyss of transition". (*Six Plays:* 144). The potential producer of the play is cautioned to ignore "the cultural clash" façade and devote all his attention to eliciting the "threnodic essence" of the play. The combination of ritual as theme and technique add up to make *Death and the King's Horseman* the most sustained example of Soyinka's ritual drama in response to which Osofisan (1978: 166) asserts:

> the play does not merely hang upon the framework of ritual: the play is the ritual itself. Techniques and theme weld fluidly to yield a theatrical experience in which both actors and audience are meant to participate, and this participation extends further beyond the province of the

emotional to the psychical, beyond mere physical exhilaration to the deeper spiritual fulfillment. The dramaturgical accent now is not on the chaos of an individual disjunction, but rather on the all-pervading personality of Iku, Death itself, celebrated like a primordial deity.

The pre-occupation of Soyinka then is to "epochalize" death and in the process, use it as an example of the concept of sacrifice and heroism or individual will. *Death and the King's Horseman* like *The Strong Breed* focuses on a communal festival at the phase of transition. The play opens and its actions revolve around the high point of the preparation of the ritual death of Elesin Oba, the king's horseman to join the Alaafin who had died thirty days earlier. The requirements of the custom as already outlined in the Bere festival and *Oba Waja* is that Elesin Oba dies to transfer his worldly company to the abyss of transition on the king's way to the world of the spirits. The consequences of a botched transition of Elesin are too clear: the king would be trapped miserably in the pathway between the earth and the ancestral world. In this state, he will rain curses on human subjects and this will have the effect of engendering immeasurable negative consequences. Nature is tossed in a state of imbalance and communal psychic dislocation would gradually tilt the world from its course.

Confronted with this fact, the Oyo people revere Elesin Oba. They turn his departure into a festival, and adorn him with the richest of traditional clothes, granting all his earthly wishes. At the climax of his farewell dance among the market women, the Elesin insists on consummating a wedding with a virgin. This decision fills the people with foreboding especially Iyaloja and the Praise-Singer whose anxieties mount as the Horseman's revelry among the women deepens:

PRAISE-SINGER: They love to spoil you but
beware. The hands of women also weaken the unwary.
In their time the great wars came and went, the white
slavers came and went, they took away the heart of our
race, they bore away the mind and muscle of our race. The

city fell and was rebuilt. Our world was never wrenched
from its course (*Six Plays*: 148).

Iyaloja's concession is premised on her spiritual role as mediator
in the ritual transition:

> ... You pray to him to serve as your intercessor to the world
> – don't set this world adrift in your own time, would you
> rather it was my hand whose sacrilege wrenched it loose?
> (161).

However, she also feels the premonition of a dulled will through
libidinous indulgence and minces no world in warning Elesin
Oba:

> ... You wish to travel light. Well the earth is yours. But be
> sure the seed you leave in it attracts no curse (162).

Elesin made a show of his enormous will in his rendition of the
story of the "Not-I-bird" and at several points in the play,
especially when he consciously recognizes the limits of worldly
honour: "Life is honour, it ends when honour ends ..." (*Six Plays*:
154).

With the concession of Iyaloja, funeral drums blend with
wedding festivities paradoxically symbolizing the ritual union of
life and death. The consummation of the wedding between Elesin
(on the threshold of ancestral ascent) and the virgin guarantees
the prospect of continuity through the unborn. This rare wedding
of the earth and the "timelessness of the ancestor" world is
announced by Elesin to Iyaloja:

> Take it. It is no mere virgin stain, but the union of life
> and the seeds of passage. My vital flow, the last from this
> flesh is intermingled with the promise of future life (180).

However, in this Ogunnian act aimed at continuity lies the initial
hubris of Elesin Oba. Elesin is expected to bridge the gulf of
transition in all its phases. Thus, after planting the seed of
continuity he is expected to perform the Promethean – Ogunnian
duty of crossing the abyss to secure passage for the dead king:

ELESIN: Our marriage is not yet wholly fulfilled. When earth andpassage wed, the consummation is complete only when there are grains of earth on the eyelids of passage (*Six Plays*: 181).

The penalty for Elesin's initial daring act is the sapping of his will with its imminent consequences of communal psychic dislocation. The intervention of the District Officer, blinded to the metaphysical import of Elesin's death further aided his failure. The world is wrenched from its true course; cosmic harmony and continuity is threatened. The ensuing confusion is represented in the failed hero's laments and excuses which centre on the alien disruption and emphasize libidinity over liminality.

However, not all the excuses in the world could save Elesin the wrath of a people whose cosmos is threatened by disharmony captured in the vituperations of Olohun-Iyo and Iyaloja:

IYALOJA: You have betrayed us. We fed you
sweetmeats such as we hoped awaited you on the other side. But you said
No, I must eat the world's left overs. We called you leader and oh, how you
led us on, What we have no intention of eating should not be held to the nose (210-211).

The result of this betrayal is tragedy for the community. Olunde returns on time to perform his ritual obligations over the "dead" Elesin, his father, only to be confronted with the shame of his father's dishonourable and disastrous hesitation. Olunde valiantly renounces his father, opting to restore honour to his household and harmony to the community by dying, thus, achieving the Ogunnian feat through the destruction of the physical self, thus bridging the gulf between the living and the dead. The son has played the father and this heightens the cause for Elesin's denigration by Iyaloja: "Elesin Oba, tell me, you who know so well the cycle of the plantain: is it the parent shoot which withers to give sap to the younger or, does your wisdom see it running the other way?" (*Six Plays*: 212).

However, even at this critical period, the machinery for continuity has been set in motion through Olunde's dynamic act of the will as the Praise-Singer points out ... "But this young shoot has poured its sap into the parent stalk and we know this is not the way of life. Our world is tumbling in the void of strangers, Elesin" (218). The only adverse implication of Elesin's death later is stressed in Iyaloja's regret:

> He is gone at last into the passage but oh, how late it all is.
> His son will feast on the meat and throw him the bones.
> The passage is clogged with droppings from the king's stallion;
> he will arrive all stained in dung (219).

The essence of this is that Elesin's death is not a ritual death. It falls short of the transcendental as he fails to "raise his will to cut the thread of life at the summons of the drum". Yet a significant aspect of the ritual drama often ignored is the import of Elesin's belated action. Though it almost spelt doom for the community, to some extent it helps ensure continuity in the chain of the contact between the living and the dead and the unborn, and implicitly in the Elesin's own lineage.

The assertion is lent credence to by the declaration of Iyaloja, the matriarchal authority and chief mediator of the ritual transition leading to the resolution of the play:

> Now forget the dead, forget even the living
> Turn your mind only to the unborn (219).

The communal assumption at this stage is that change has taken place and cosmic harmony has been restored on the metaphysical level. Viewed within the perspective of ritual as communication strategy however, the play can be seen in terms of Ropo Sekoni's (1987: 85) definition of ritual as a "sequence of discrete, enacted events usually combined in a stereotyped manner and designed to produce a special effect on both actors and spectators ..."

Death and the King's Horseman has been divided into five acts or sequences of enactments. In the first Elesin is seen in a ritualistic consummation of a wedding with his new bride, the outcome of which is suspended until the third act. The second act enacts Pilkings and wife's preparation for the evening's ball costumed in an ancestral masque; the import of this act of desecration is heightened by the differing reaction of Amusa and the other natives. The third has three subsections explicating characters in situations of conscious ritual acting. First is the cosmic scene of the ridicule of the native colonial agents – Amusa and his men – by the girls (176-179); the second returns us to the act commenced in the first, now yielding "the union of life and seeds of passage but still incomplete. The last section of the third act completes the main ritual of the play initiated in the first act, that of the Elesin's summoning of his will to terminate his life as the moon attains a specified maturity. Here the rhythm creates a sense of distance as Elesin assumes a trance-like state.

Perhaps for theatrical similitude of this enactment we could rely on Lois Adams' notes taken during rehearsals and performances of the play at the Goodman Theatre in Chicago to supplement the scanty stage directions of the text. According to Adams (1980:151-152) as Elesin's Praise-Singer reminds him of the importance of his duty and offers to help through the transitory passage, the lights dim. Elesin's voice grows drowsy, his step heavier, and his trance deepens. The women pick up a long white cloth meanwhile and hold it as they all dance round in a circle. The cloth flutters over Elesin with Iyaloja's chant of the "It takes an Elesin to die the death of death ..." lines at the end of which the white cloth is lifted over Elesin's head symbolizing that he has passed over to the other side of existence, and left the community of the living.

The impact of this act settles on the audience, the ritual moves into Act 4 – the Residence, setting of the ball organized for the royal visitor from England. An intermingling of the two worlds imminent at this point builds up the conflict and its tragic dimensions as Pilkings is alerted to go and halt Elesin's almost complete journey into the abyss. Finally, the last act links the first and in fact recalls it, though now under contrasting conditions. The location has shifted from the market place to Pilking's convertible prison; denigration has replaced veneration and a proposed ritual transition almost becomes mere tragic suicide.

However, of all the acts and sub-sections, four of Soyinka's dramaturgic departure from the historical material stands out in bringing out the ritual at the centre of the play. They have been outlined by Biodun Jeyifo (1985:52) thus: "Elesin Oba's marriage to the young maiden; the visit of the Prince; Olunde's sojourn in and timely return from Britain, and lastly the suicide of Elesin." Since we have elucidated on almost all the segments, we shall focus now mainly on the dramatic significance of Soyinka's placement of the actions of the play two years back and Olunde's sojourn in England. First, it helps Soyinka to explore and reinforce his treatment of the concept of individual will, self-sacrifice and heroism by placing it within a universal context. Secondly, it aided Soyinka's ideological battle in insisting that the European worldview or philosophy of life is not necessarily superior to that of traditional Africa. Both concerns get succinct expression in the dialogue between Olunde and Jane.

The two years by which Soyinka sets back the dramatic action place Olunde in the middle of the world war. From this vantage point, Soyinka is able to press the point that the so called ritual practice of 1946 Oyo is no more barbaric than the pogrom of the Second World War which Olunde witnesses and indirectly takes part in, in 1944. Through the subject matter of Olunde and Jane's discussion which compares the captain's self-sacrifice with Elesin's ritual sacrifice, Soyinka portrays the concept of heroism and self-will for communal regeneration in a universal light. Jane's remark about the blown-up ship ignites Olunde's curiosity and provokes his perceptive response to the issue.

> OLUNDE: Do you mean through enemy action?
> JANE: Oh no, the war hasn't come that close ....
> The captain blew himself up with it. Deliberately. Simon

said someone had to remain on board to light the fuse
There was no other way to save lives. Fancy welcoming
you back with such morbid news.
OLUNDE: I don't find the news morbid at all. I find it
rather inspiring. It is an affirmative commentary on life.
JANE: What is?
OLUNDE: That captain's self-sacrifice (*Six Plays:* 192-193).

This way, Soyinka reveals that the hubristic act of the Captain is
a dynamic act of self-sacrifice and dramatically fore-shadows
Olunde's ultimate Promethean act. Subtly, the acts of both
Ogunnian characters are projected as being less barbaric than
the mass killings during the war. The emerging import of Soyinka's
use of ritual communicational strategies therefore is that it
reinforces his metaphysical objectives. Our position finds
expression in the summation provided on Soyinka's ritual theatre
by Jahnheiz Jahn (1986:253) thus: "while the dramatic structure
moves from ritual to masque and from mimicry to irony and
repetition, it also helps elicit the metaphysical meaning through
this structure."

Finally, we shall now focus on a fundamental aspect of the
ritual dramaturgy employed in *Death and the King's Horseman*.
This is the aesthetics of ritual language. The play is couched,
steeped and sauced right out of Yoruba mythology and folklore.
At the level of ordinary conversation, the play is suffused with
home spun images taken from the African heritage to facilitate
effective communication with the audience and ensure a kind of
cultural continuity at the intellectual level. Home-made images
and metaphors make the exchanges between the Elesin Oba and
his Praise-Singer a delight right from its opening:

PRAISE SINGER: Elesin O! Elesin Oba! Howu!
What tryst is this the Cockerel goes to keep with
such haste that he must leave his tail behind?
ELESIN: (Slows down a bit, laughing).
A tryst where the cockerel needs no adornment.

As the play progresses, its language wades deeper into Yoruba literary and cultic traditions filled with proverbs, riddles, praise poems and panegyrics and other elliptic references which become its main dramatic device. Thus, Elesin captivates the audience with his expertise in mime and mimicry as he dances out the story of the "Not – I bird" to show his enormous strength of will. This emerges at the end after Elesin's satiric presentation of the Priests, Aafa, Courtesan and sundry as they escape in panic at the sight of the "Not-I bird":

> I, when that Not-I bird perched upon
> my roof, bade him seek his nest again
> safe, without care or fear. I unrolled
> my welcome mat for him to see. Not–I
> flew happily away, you'll hear his voice
> No more in this life time – You all know
> what I am (*Six Plays:* 152).

To keep Elesin's spirit in ascent for his task, lyrical praise chants and the Oriki flows steadily from the Praise-Singer:

> I say you are that who chanced
> upon the calabash of honour you
> thought it was palmwine, drained its contents
> to the final drop (154).

However, as Elesin gets nearer to the commencement of his journey through the abyss, ordinary praise chants gave way to a fusion of language and music as the Praise-Singer attains his highest lyrical heights. The Praise-Singer progressively becomes "the mouth piece of the mythopoeic forces" (*Myth, Literature:* 148). In fact, at a point the spirit of the King lurking in the abyss overtook him:

> PRAISE-SINGER: Elesin Alaafin, can you hear my voice
> ELESIN: Faintly, my friend, faintly.
> PRAISE-SINGER: Elesin Alaafin, can you hear my call?
> ELESIN: Faintly, my king, faintly
> PRAISE-SINGER: Is your memory sound, Elesin?
>   Shall my voice be a blade of grass and

	Tickle the armpit of the past?
ELESIN:	My memory needs no prodding but what do you wish to say to me?...
PRAISE-SINGER:	If you cannot come, I said, Swear. You'll tell my favourite horse. I shall ride on through the gates alone ... (182).

These exhortations of the last moments to Elesin are done against the background of the "swaying votaries" of "the fourth stage" (*Myth, Literature:* 148) which registers in Elesin's mind as the women with their ritual dirge sung to regal motions and solemn as gentle accompaniment to the main dialogue:

"Ale le lo, awo mi lo: (182).

Words at these crucial moments are taken back to their roots as the three worlds meet in the threshold of transition, visible in the incantations of Iyaloja:

It is the death of war that kills the
Valiant. It takes an Elesin to die
the death of death ... Only Elesin ...
the unknowable death of death ... dies
Graceful, graceful does the horseman regain
The stables at the end of day, graceful ... (184).

Prologue and dialogue in *Death and the King's Horseman* go on as a succession of questions and answers, with elliptical references to such transcendental elements called the numinous essence by Soyinka like the cult of "Osugbo" the dirge cult of "gbedu" – the sacred royal drum and other ritualistic terms all in combination aimed at summoning Elesin to a trance-like state when he loses consciousness. *Death and the King's Horseman* is a ritual dance whose climax is a fusion of nuptial drums and funeral dance. The dance culminates in the death of the promethean Olunde and the failed hero Elesin. We end with a celebrative theatre through a ritual process, a communal act which results in a collective experience of actors and audience utilizing mime, music, dance and mask, thus confirming Soyinka's use of ritual as metaphysical, communication and aesthetic strategies to defeat the limitations of the proscenium stage. His success in doing this is what Izevbaye (1988:60) points out when he says:

> For Soyinka, the kind of theatre which seeks to recreate the physical conditions of traditional festival theatre is not the only medium favourable for the audience. The proscenium barrier can be crossed if the playwright treats the modern theatre as "two functioning halves of the same dynamic". The dramatic is thus a mediation between audience and performance and direct operation of moral and sensual forces.

From the insights provided by the above, it is useful to conclude this chapter by establishing the contrasts existing between *The Strong Breed* and *Death and the King's Horseman*. While both treat the larger issues of communal regeneration through the concepts of individual will, scapegoatism and self-sacrifice using the medium of communal ritual celebration, there exists striking differences in the theatrical strategies employed in both plays. Femi Osofisan (1978:165) has earlier on drawn our attention to some of these differences.

First of all, *The Strong Breed* is more of a "tragedy of individual limitation" whose framework hangs largely on borrowed elements of classical Western theatrical histrionics of tragedy. The highlighters of these are: the conscious absence of violence on stage, reports of Eman's death conveyed only through the stage directions; there is also an emphasis on the non-presentation of the comic or the vulgar so as not to taint the serious subject-matter of tragedy. Lastly, a kind of distance exists between the audience and the actors, the audience being passive observers of the activities on stage.

The ritual impulse is felt in the play as pointed out earlier on in the interpolation of the chronological sequences of the play through flashbacks showing the background of Eman as a member of a family of carriers and the various rituals which explain his involvement in the present one. However, all these limitations do not exist in *Death and the King's Horseman* as detailed analysis have shown.

In terms of subject-matter, two different pictures of the communities examined in both plays also emerge to prove Soyinka's philosophy emphasizing the morality of the individuals and the generality in the society for the achievement and maintenance of communal harmony. However, the failure of Soyinka's tragic heroes in both plays can be likened to that of Ogun at the battle of Ire, a vehicle of communal regeneration and awareness which the playwright explains thus:

> The community emerges from ritual experience "charged with new strength for action" because of the protagonist's Promethean raid of the durable resources of the transitional realm, immersed with it, he is enabled empathically to transmit its essence to the choric participants of the rites - the community *(Myth, Literature and the African World:* 33).

3

RITUAL AS FRAMEWORK IN THE DRAMA OF THE RETURNING CYCLE

Cannibalism as an imagery for the artistic portrayal of the endless evil of homo sapiens the world over has been a consistent feature of Soyinka's utterances and dramatic output from the early stages of his career. This imagery runs through the tragic triad – *A Dance of the forests*, *The Road* and *Madmen and Specialists* which we shall be examining in this chapter. In an interview he granted Lewis Nkosi shortly after a London performance of *A Dance of the Forests*, Soyinka admitted that one of the central concerns in the conception of the play was; "the realization that human beings are just destructive, that human beings are simply cannibals all over the world, so that their main preoccupation seems to be eating up another" (Duerden and Pieterse, 1972:173).

This terrifying statement has led to what Mowah (1981:63) describes as the artist's "prescient experience" entailing mainly a tragic and pessimistic vision informed by his conviction that the ugly situation in Africa is reflective of the state of affairs in the universe in general. Worse still, it has been so from the fount of humanity. Probably influenced by this vision of humanity is the theory of tragedy formulated by the playwright. We enumerated the main characteristics of these tragic postulations in chapter one.

However, its highlight is that tragedy has its roots in the primordial anguish initiated by the fragmentation of the original essence leading to the epic move of the struggle of the gods to reunite with men, a struggle which failed, thus engendering the need for ritual sacrifice to stem the annual rupture of anguish in the human realm. As hinted earlier on, the transposition of this theory within sociopolitical contexts in drama has given birth to plays which are both contemporary and metaphysical at one breath. But Soyinka's preoccupation with the contemporary is not merely the depiction of mankind's tragedy. They encapsulate exorcism and exposition of the precipitating factors of "the total collapse of ideals" with the glimmer of optimistic hopes for change. Against this background, Soyinka's concern in the tragic triad can be said to be three.

First is the metaphysical which Moore (1972:35) has described as Soyinka's "profound concern for the way in which the gods manifest their will both through human acts and the contingent moulding of human personality." Second is the unsparing portrayal of man as a cannibal whose manifestations are visible in his graft, corruption, moral bankruptcy, injustice and a penchant for bloodshed in the world. The third is the direct offshoot of the second – the satire of the depicted follies of mankind.

A prevalent current of critical concerns on the identified plays of Soyinka is an exclusive focus on either the metaphysical as seen in the analysis of Salt (1976:114-127) or the sociopolitical perspective alone as done by Jeyifo (1985:11-22). This is apparently borne out of the failure to recognize a fundamental theoretical standpoint of Soyinka's that the African sensibility incorporates without distinction, the political, economic, historical and metaphysical aspects of life. Thus, ultimately, questions of transition and continuity could still be found at the roots of these three plays just as in the first two in chapter two. However, while ritual constitutes the subjects and technique in both *The Strong Breed* and *Death and the King's Horseman,* it functions as mere formal framework for metaphysical, thematic, communica-tional and aesthetic strategies in the tragic triad as our explications will presently show.

A Dance of the Forests

Ropo Sekoni (1987:85) places this first major play of Soyinka at the edge of the continuum in Soyinka's ritual drama in which he uses "the invocation of Egungun" as a motivating force for the main action in the play. Going a step further, Osofisan (1978:494-5), citing the authority of Joel Adedeji, establishes that *A Dance of the Forests* is constructed like the funeral masques of the primordial times. Historically, the funeral masques came about when a lineage group perennially invoked the spirit of their dead progenitors who emerge from the bowels of the earth in a mask symbol to bless and admonish the bereaved. One year in the 18th Century, during the reign of Alaafin Ofinran, a court official called Ologbin Ologbojo and another member of the Egungun cult contrived to convert the practice into a festival by directing all lineage groups to bring their dead out on the same occasion. The mask symbols duly appeared and in processions accompanied by singing crowds of their descendants moved to the royal palace. A further innovation came towards the end of the procession when each of the masks was called up to dance for the king. This later led to a competition and a seasonal event which metamorphosed into a communal theatre.

Soyinka in *A Dance of the Forests* has used this masquerade motif in dramatizing the human condition. The play entails a warning to the people to beware of complacency as they celebrate the rite of passage from colonialism to independence at the "Gathering of the Tribes" for which it was originally commissioned. *A Dance of the Forests* opens in a community where the prevailing mood is one of celebration of a major festival involving the three components of the continuum: the human, the ancestors, and the gods guarding over the community. The nature of the festival is the procession, like in our example, of the dead towards the square at the heart of the human community. However, a quick departure is soon made from this seeming faithful adherence to the festival replica. An occasion of the above magnitude deserves the presence of only the noblest and inspiring of the ancestors, and this the human community requested to sanction the festival. But to their chagrin, they are sent two wretched individuals whose emergence immediately evokes communal guilt stemming from the violent death of the ancestors in the past which is a painful reminder of their unending acts of self-deception and self-destruction. Frightened by this thwarted expectation, the humans denounce this testimony of their past and summarily eject them.

The gods, witnessing the treatment of their chosen "obscenities" decide to intervene. They elect to invite the Dead ones to their midst to dance for them. Furthermore, disguised as Obaneji, the Forest Father, being Soyinka's representation of Olodumare or Obatala, also decides to arrange the presence of selected members of the human community who were linked with the Dead Ones in the present generation. Having prodded the three guilty mortals – Demoke, Rola and Adenebi – to accept a movement "deeper" into the forest, dramatic action shifts to the chthonic realm, thus signaling the beginning of the physical interaction of both the metaphysical and sociological characters in the play to use the terms of Adedeji (1987:107).

So far two dramaturgic manipulations have taken place to transform the opening mood of celebration to the realm of metaphysical experience. The summoned ancestors move into the forest rather than the village square. Secondly, guilty relatives rather than joyous celebrants accompany them. Once deep in the forest, Forest Head causes the mortals to confess their crimes thus creating, "a kind of purgatorial mass in which the characters are led one by one to confess their guilt and recognize themselves for who they are". (Osofisan: 1987, 494). Soon afterwards in a third dramaturgic manipulation or enactment and a well executed flash-back scene, Forest Head confronts them with a picture of the past where these same characters as functionaries of Mata Kharibu's court commit similar crimes as the present ones confessed. The human protagonists were key resurgents from the past.

Adenebi both in the past and present remains an embodiment of the corruption in the body politic of the country. As a historian he distorts the past and deliberately misinterprets history to please Kharibu and justify his war. Beneath the façade of respectability which makes him denounce the company of Rola, the notorious courtesan, is concealed a rotten interior which permits his involvement in the demonic deal enabling the sale of self-assertive soldiers in the court of Mata Kharibu (*Collected Plays* 1:54) and the event of the "incineration"scandal in his present position as councillor to which he implicitly confesses following the prodding of Forest Father. Adenebi's insensitivity makes him negate the very essence of African traditional values of hospitability. Thus, his support for the Old Man's proposition for the invitation of the ancestors is not motivated by its unifying essence but by the grandeur of self-deception concealed in empty rhetoric:

> Let them symbolize all that is noble in our nation. Let them be our
> historical link for the season of rejoicing. Warriors. Sages.
> Conquerors. Builders. Philosophers. Mystics. Let us assemble them
> round the totem of their resurrected glory (*Collected Plays I*: 31).

However, in spite of himself, Soyinka uses his flowing rhetoric to make ironic statements on the bleak hope of humanity as could be seen in his advocacy of war without justification:

> War is the only consistency that past
> Ages afford us. It is the legacy which new nations seek to
> perpetuate.
> Patriots are grateful for wars.
> Soldiers have never questioned bloodshed.
> The cause is always the accident, your majesty, and war
> is Destiny ... (Collected Plays I :51).

Rola both in her present and past existence as courtesan extraordinaire is void of human compassion. Thus, she excuses her pernicious destruction of countless men as an ordinary act of commerce:

> What is it to me? When your businessmen
> Ruin the lesser one, do you go crying
> to them? I also have no pity for the
> one who invested foolishly. Investors,
> that is all they ever were to me (24).

With this remorseless stance, her special role in Mata Kharibu's court as the source of many a man's death and potential threat to universal peace becomes not totally surprising. For the pursuit of a canary, soldiers and servants could die:

> COURT POET: Did not a soldier fall to
>   his death from the roof
>   two days ago, my lady?
> MADAME TORTOISE: That is so. I heard a disturbance
>   and I called the guard to find
>   the cause. I thought it came
>   from the roof and I directed
>   him there. He was too eager
>   and fell (Collected Plays I: 47).

Like Adenebi, he is anxious to sever traditional family links. Her inability to seduce the warrior to a destructive engagement leads to her condemnation of the dead ones.

Thus, the dead women presenting her case before Forest Head places Madame Tortoise outside womanhood because she possesses no quality of that sex:

QUESTIONER: Who sent you?
DEAD WOMAN: I am certain she had no womb,
              But I think it was a woman (60).

Demoke, the last one from the human community undergoing trial is both in the past and the present an artist, a fait which clearly makes him the Ogunnian character. He posses the creative destructive nature of Ogun as well as other human contradictions like jealousy, hatred and spitefulness. Demoke, the carver in the present is asked to carve a totem as a symbol of the festival for the Gathering of the Tribes. He pleads ignorant of the fact that the tree is in the sacred grove of Oro. For this sacrilege Esuoro, Soyinka's combination of the spirit of the trickster god Esu and the god of death Oro, is angry and is seeking revenge against Demoke. However, Demoke has acted in compliance with the guidance of his patron-god Ogun, who is sworn to protect his servant thus provoking a conflict in the ancestral world and proving the fallibility of even the gods. However, a greater manifestation of Demoke's destructive nature which further deepens the crisis in the cosmic realm is the death of Esuoro's servant Oremole while carving the totem. Under the probings of the Forest Father and the unsettling presence of the Dead Ones, Demoke confesses that the apprentice did not fall accidentally but was murdered in a moment of envy stirred by Ogunnian possession because he reached a higher height to carve the totem which he (Demoke) could not.

DEMOKE: ... I plucked him down!
Demoke's head is no woman's cloth, spread to receive wood shavings from a carpenter ...

This act of destruction yields creativity seen in the inspired skill and speed producing the totems:

... Alone I cut the strands that mocked me, till head and

boastful slave lay side by side, and I Demoke, sat in the shoulders of the tree, My spirit set free and singing. My father's hands possessed by demons of blood. And I carved through days and nights till tools were blunted, and these hands, my father's hands swelled big as the tree-trunk (27).

For this act of hubris a penance has to be extracted.

After the exposure of the human sins of the past and the present, attempts at previewing the future made up the last two enactments through the Forest Father's offering of a chance of cleansing and a new beginning by the performance of the Dance of the "Half-Child" and Dance of the "Unwilling Sacrifice". The recourse to dances as a means of resolving the complex conflicts in the play has been remarked as being nothing short of the bewildering by Ogunba (1975:98) and Mahood (1966:16-33). However, the dances are plausible enough as resolutions within the context of the situation of the dramatic action. We are no longer in the village square or the Oba's palace but in the thick of the chthonic realm, hence events just as we see in the dances can no longer take place on the level of the plainly realistic. Thus, the journey in the chthonic realm becomes a physical actualization of the psychic journey usually made by the tragic protagonists with which communicants or ritual participants empathize through vicarious experience. Through this technique, the human community came in contact with beings that "lie guardian to the gulf" who are dissatisfied with the conduct of man's bloody thirsty and pernicious nature. The spirit of the palm, as possessor of the life giving sap predicts blood instead of nourishment because of man's "blackened hearts".

> White skeins wove me. I, spirit
> of the Palm – Now course
> I red.
> I who suckle blackened hearts,
> know Heads will fall down,
> Crimson in their red (64).

The other spirits – the Sun, Darkness, Precious Stones and others are also full of foreboding of evil emanating from man's vindictive nature and the pollution of life giving sources turned into agents of death. Thus, this cosmic disharmony coupled with the searing conflict between Esuoro and Ogun places the fate of the Half-Child the symbolic representation of the new nation's future in danger as all the forces seek vengeance on it. The picture of the endangered future is vividly presented in the dance in which the Half-Child is tossed between Esuoro, his jester and the triplets. It takes only the daring act of Demoke, the creative artist aided by Ogun to rescue the child. However, this seeming redeeming act opens up new anxieties since he stands confused with the Half-Child. A decision to hold on to it could have broken the cycle of tragedy but the gods will not permit it because, "... it is no light matter to reverse the deed that was begun many lives ago ..." (71).

Glimmers of the new beginnings could be seen in the "chastened" look of the erstwhile courtesan – Rola and in Demoke's question on the relevance of additional sacrifices of expiation suggested by the Old Man:

> DEMOKE: Expiation? We three who lived many lives in this one night, have we not done enough? Have we not felt enough for the memory of our remaining lives? (73).

Whether history proves Demoke right or wrong becomes the subject of Soyinka's two subsequent tragedies as we shall see in due course.

Soyinka in this play employs an ingenious ritual form which converts his theoretical postulations which is mainly psychical into physical, visible actions on the stage. The psychic journey of the tragic protagonist is replaced by the physical journey of the communicants or the community into the forest through a series of ritual enactments capable of eliciting empathy from ritual participants and the audience especially at the anguished scenes of the humans during the dances. Language in *A Dance of the Forests* becomes a ritual in itself – highly stylized, formulaic and a means of identifying the peculiarities of character's role. Thus while Aroni's language is mainly poetic, evoking the riddles of the spirit of Wisdom that he is, that of the Forest Head disguised as Obaneji oscillates between ironic cynicism and boredom stemming from the distress of his knowledge.

The language of the other metaphysical characters especially the spirits are also highly poetic. However, that of the Dirge-man and Agboreko draws directly from the rituals of oracular poetry

DIRGE-MAN: Move on eyah! Move apart
I felt the wind breathe – no more keep away
now. Leave the dead some room to dance ...

AGBOREKO: Have you seen a woman throw away
Her pestle when she really means to pound yam?
When Iredade took her case to Orunmila, he said,
If the worm doesn't jig near roost, the fowl may still want
to peck
Go home therefore, go home. Iredade turned sadly ...
away (36-37).

Soyinka's pre-occupation with ritual as aesthetic strategy becomes pronounced when, in the opening scene of the second part of the play, we witness the Crier's mechanical to and fro movement to announce the ritual enactment of the past:

... Sons and subjects of Forest Father, and all that
dwell in his domain', take note, this night is the
welcome of the dead. When spells are cast and dead
invoked by the living, only such may resume their body
corporeal as are summoned. When the understreams
that whirl them endlessly complete a cycle ... We hold these
rites, at human insistence. By proclamation, let the mists
of generations be now dispersed. Forest Father,
unveil, unveil the phantasmagoria of protagonists
from the dead (45).

The Road, like A Dance of the Forests, is constructed upon the ritual framework of a masque but now specifically on the model of the "agemo" masque, "the religious cult of flesh dissolution." The play, written in 1965, was influenced by the contemporary realities of the Nigerian society of the 1960s especially in the second half of the decade when social and spiritual decadence, corruption and moral bankruptcy precipitated the civil war and its accompanying harrowing experience. Thus, the play doubles as a social satire and a metaphysical examination of the nature of death as a means of valuing its complementary parity, life and stemming attenuating threats against it.

Both concerns revolve around the quasi-mystical protagonist, Professor and his "part psychic, part intellectual grope ... towards the essence of death". He attempts an understanding of the knowledge of the Forest Head in *A Dance of Forest* encapsulated in the "Word" through the medium of the road and its various dimensions. Thus, two concepts are important to the understanding of the play; the "word" and the "road".

Oyin Ogunba (1975:125) defines the word as "a name used in the play to cover a number of codes for apprehending the universe in Professor's society". Izevbaye (1976:53) drawing attention to the play's concern with death, describes the road as the essential link between "the spiritual and the satirical aspects of the play by being the agent of death as well as the path along which the dead passengers are carried to their church funeral." Corruption is the bane of the society in which Professor conducts his search as epitomized in both his own character and the methodology of his work. Thus, the critical point is that while the society is constantly aware of the knowledge of death and is covered by it as a threat to continuity, corruption and spiritual sterility present an ability to contain or, at least, curtail its effects. Hence , what we continue to have is a cycle of tragedies from the roads and a deepening psychic fear of death. A forcible attempt at confronting it through sacrilegious means only results in tragedy as Professor's fate shows. Within this perspective, both the metaphysical and the material are linked in *The Road* as further explications will demonstrate.

The atmosphere of the play itself effectively communicates

the playwright's concern with the metaphysical subjects of death and transition as noted by Izevbaye (1976s53). This has been created through ritual communicational strategies like language as well as verbal and non-verbal stage icons. For example in the opening situation, the stage directions indicate the graveyard in the background, the sleepy forms of the layabouts, the spiders, and Samson's attraction to them.

Thus, even before any speech in the play, a lot of non-verbal symbolism has helped in launching the audience into the realm of ritual expectations: dawn is barely breaking; a lopsided mammy wagon is thrusting down stage', there is an initial silence which almost makes the shack an extension of the graveyard, especially with Murano's stealthy departure. Significant also is the inscription on the dismantled wagon now Professor's "AKSIDENT STORE" for spare parts. Furthermore, the symbolic relevance of the striking clock is a signification of time's uncontrollable passage. It has a visible frightening effect on Samson the only tout awake when it strikes, and forms the subject of Salubi's musings about the inescapabillty of human existence from time:

> Six o'clock I bet. I don't know how it
> Is, but no matter when I go to sleep,
> I wake up when it strikes six ...
> (*Collected Plays I*: 152)

This is followed shortly by Professor's postulations which centre on man and his inevitable destiny in the hands of death:

> There are dangers in the Quest I know,
> but the Word may be found companion
> not to life but Death (*Collected Plays I*: 159).

All these serve to establish the extension of Soyinka's concern beyond the objective socio-political milieu within which the dramatis persona operate. This is reinforced by the conscious avoidance of concrete references to settings and historical events. However, through what appears like common place exchanges and caricatures, the play draws and deals with the contemporary through Samson and Salubi. Both expose the identities (past and present) of the personae that are not physically present, their work, their positions in society, their fears and more consciously their misdemeanours. Through their antics the audience gets an insight into the unjust social stratification in the society and the records of corruption staining Professor's past, and questions the real intent behind his present pre-occupation.

As a respected lay-reader in the church, Professor abuses his office by pilfering church funds but the system, especially the law and the society's regard for the elite shields him. Salubi is given a thorough lesson when he inquires after the outcome of Professor's misappropriation:

> SAMSON: You think they just put somebody in prison like that? Professor his very self?
> Of course you don't know your history. When Professor entered church, everybody turned
> round and the eyes of the congregation followed him to his pew – and he had his own
> private pew. Let me tell you, and if a stranger went and sat in it, the church warden wasted
> no time in driving him out.
> SALUBI: Dat one no to church, na high society.
> SAMSON: You no sabbe de ting man de call class so shurrup your mout. Professor enh he get class ... (162).

On his excommunication from the church, Professor, still hiding under the cloak of his status perpetrates criminal acts like forgery, and robbery at accident points which he causes deliberately in the name of his search, and to gather spare parts for his Aksident Store. All these are done as later enactments by the layabouts will show through the connivance of Particulars Joe, a corrupt law enforcement officer who spends more time with the layabouts in the shack. Furthermore, through the encounters with the layabouts and lower characters, Chief-in-Town, a member of the political elite is exposed as a corrupt, selfish opportunist who uses the thugs to maintain the status quo. Samson's rebuttal of the Chief's shady business in the shack constitutes Soyinka's indictment of the latter's class.

> CHIEF: Captain
> SAMSON: (without turning around) They've all gone.
> CHIEF: How long ago did they leave?...
> SAMSON: No idea.
> CHIEF: You are new around here. Are you one
> of the boys?
> SAMSON: I won't thug for you if that's what you mean
> (167-168).

Thus, corruption entrenched in the body politic of the country and other socio-political realities like irresponsible governance, poverty, ignorance and violence are castigated in the society. This decadence that informs Soyinka's probing of the spiritual, moral, and psychological state has also been encroached upon by the sacrilegeous practices of the likes of Professor. To do this, the play dwells on the intricacies of threats to continuity whose ultimate power is death and the prevalent fear of it expressed through the different characters at various levels. This constitutes the principal source of the ritual evocations in the play, since the patron god of the drivers and the layabouts in the transport business is Ogun – the creative-destructive god.

In spite of the closeness of the drivers' and touts' profession to death, its fear nonetheless remains an intrinsic part of the make-up of the main characters, especially Samson. Thus when Professor offers to go and show Salubi "a scene of madness where a motor car throws itself against a tree – Gbram ! And showers of crystal flying on broken soul" (159), Samson suddenly abandons his play acting to ask, "What! What was that about an accident?" (159). And to further postulations on death by Professor and his final invitation to the scene, Samson frightfully declines saying: "No thank you very much. I don't willingly seek out unpleasant sights." (159). Also reflective of his fear is his fervent plea to Kotonu: " kill us a dog, Kotonu, kill us a dog before the hungry god lies in wait and makes a substitute of me" (198).

His fear is representative of the communal apprehension often shown in the play's propitiation festivals of Ogun and the driver's dirge throughout the play. Though the songs contain lewd references reflective of the driver's characters in the main, they remind drivers of the dangers of excessive speeding on the road, an artistic and social concern of Soyinka:

> It's a long road to heaven
> It's a long road to heaven, Driver
> Go easy a – ah go easy driver
> It's a long road to heaven
> My creator, be not harsh on me ... (231).

Communal apprehension is also often expressed through respect for phenomenal metaphors like the road and timber both of which are believed to possess essences in the African metaphysical worldview as outlined earlier on in our theoretical explications. Thus, Samson in spite of his comic disposition prays, "... May we never walk when the road waits, famished ..." (165) while earlier on, Say Tokyo Kid speaks of a "hundred spirits in every guy of timber trying to do you down cause you've trapped them in ..." (171). Again, silence falls on the company at the shack as the hearse bearing the latest accident victims arrives for burial. The entire scene casts both physical and symbolic shadow on the characters:

> (An increasing rumble of metallic wheels
> on stone. The layabouts, recognizing the
> meaning, become newly sobered, take off
> their caps in respect. Kotonu has leapt up,
> staring in the direction of the noise.) ...
> (The black side of a lorry moves slowly
> past, blotting out the interior of the shack
> with its shadow ...) (192).

Thus, in one way or the other, and to varying degrees, characters in *The Road* are, by virtue of their professional engagements, protagonists of continuity, constantly aware of the Ogunnian presence irrespective of their bold exterior facades.

Five characters are more conscious of this than the others: Samson, Kotonu, Say Tokyo Kid, Murano and Professor. Samson and his talkative demonstrations have already been talked about. Kotonu the driver actually gets into a state of Ogunnian possession once. His lorry knocked down Murano (as the lead worshipper and masked figure of the driver's Ogun festival) and to escape the violent reactions of the enraged worshippers, Kotonu donned the Egungun outfit. The blood of the accident victim got into his eyes, his intense fear and frenzy led to a state of possession and a fleeting glimpse of transition. This experience makes him to abandon the road and makes him discuss the falsity of his rationalizations that extra care and sheer expertise, and not any metaphysical being could prevent road accidents, an assumption which had hitherto prevented him from killing a dog as requested by Samson.

Say Tokyo Kid's awareness, on the other hand, of the Word and Ogunnian presence is visible in his absolute belief in the talisman which he feels for "around his neck and brings out." (171). He is faithfully assured that this talisman would rescue him from the mysterious spirits of the timber trying to do him down and beyond this as Ogunba (1972:141) suggests a source of protection in "these days of political upheaval when thugs of rival political parties are said to fight not only with guns and cutlasses but also with juju power". Through this delusion he is able to contain the knowledge of his vulnerability and its psychic effects. Murano is a more obvious protagonist of transition. Knocked down in a state of Ogunnian possession, he remains in limbo, having been nursed to that effect by Professor.

He is Soyinka's "Alagemo" hanging between life and death. His resurrection is the ultimate catalyst of Professor's demise.

However, Professor is the major embodiment of the Ogunnian dare. In his selfish, self-chosen pre-occupation, he is the most conscious affront to transition. He seeks to consciously glean the guarded secrets of this fearful, numinous realm, and in the process declares "boldly":

I held a god captive, that his hands
held out the day's communion!
And should I not hope with him, to
Cheat, to anticipate the final
Confrontation, learning its nature
baring its skulking face.
(*Collected Plays II*: 224).

This hubristic confrontation he pays for with his life at the
frenzied climax of the play for neither him nor his society
possesses the moral or spiritual justification to seek the word as
pointed out earlier on. The church from which he started the
search is a congregation of the hypocritical, as well as the arrogant
and ignorant in the society. The road which he moves to is an all
embracing avenue for cannibalism through senseless killings,
corruption and negligence. Finally, the drinking shack he resorts
to in search of the word is the abode of the rejects of the road,
drivers and touts as well as bribe-seeking policemen and violent
politicians all of whom, though afraid of death, lack the will to
honestly confront it. As remarked earlier on, Professor himself is
morally unqualified for his pre-occupation since he employs both
fair and foul means in his search.

Thus, his desperation to conclude the search forcibly results
in the conflict in the last enactment of the play in which Professor
invokes the ritual dance of the Egungun out of season. This
immediately ruptures the cosmic harmony of the driver's
community, drawing protests from them, the layabouts and the
touts confronted with a threatened cosmos:

SALUBI: (trying to sneak out): No one
           is playing around with my sanity,
PROFESSOR: Let no one move ...
PARTIC JOE: Professor, you know I am not superstitious...
           But this, I swear sir, I would sooner
           you forged a hundred insurance policies.
PROF: I must hope, even now, I cannot
           yet believe that death's revelation must
           be total, or not at all.

SAY T: I reckoned this has gone too far. I ain't
          scared like all these people so I'm telling
          you, you're fooling around where you ain't
          got no business... I'm Say Tokyo Kid and I
          don't give you one damn! (226).

Totally engrossed in "The Fourth Stage", Professor heeds no warning from the drivers as the Egungun's ritual dance attains a climax. Say Tokyo Kid, now uncontrollably frightened, stabs Professor. He is in turn wounded by the resurrected Agemo. Professor gains knowledge of death only when he experiences it hence he cannot use it. However, he is able to stutter out a message which stresses the fact of the supremacy of death over all and the futility of questing for the meaning of life unprepared:

Be even like the road itself... spread a
broad sheet for death with the length
and the time of the sun between you
until the one face multiplies and the
one shadow is cast by all the doomed.
Breathe like the road, be even like
the road itself ... (229).

There is no discernible plot which could have given *The Road* a linear progression. The play, like *A Dance of the Forests,* operates through a series of enactments in which ritual is realized by communicational and aesthetic strategies through verbal and non-verbal icons, symbolic setting, the mask motif, different kinds of dialogue and extensive use of music and mime to achieve effects. A major proportion of events that culminate in the present conflicts have taken place at various times before the play itself commences, hence audience members are fed these details through recollected narrations and enactments.

The bulk of these recollections and linkages are effected by Samson and Salubi as they exchange banter and in the process enact essential past and present realities about other dead colleagues, themselves and most importantly about Professor and details of his past. Many of the present events are directly traceable to the past, hence, through a constant use of the flashback technique, and recalls, both often merge thus giving the impression of Soyinka's concept of time as a cyclical continuum. At times, even seemingly unconnected present events and enactments from the past are merged. For example, without any preceding notifica-tions or cues, the audience is plunged into the enactment of the scene in which Murano is knocked down by Kotonu's lorry:

> PROF:　Do let me know if you hear anything...
> 　　　　about the matter of the church
> 　　　　fund ...
> SAMSON: ...Yes sir, yes sir...
> PROF:　Up the aisle with them and
> 　　　　the chancellery. Don't let their
> 　　　　cassock deter you, the eagle
> 　　　　sides with me, we will do
> 　　　　battle, but first, we must
> 　　　　find the Word...
> SAMSON: Oh yes sir, of course, Professor.
> PROF:　For the day will come, oh yes
> 　　　　it will. Even atonement wilts
> 　　　　before the word ...
> 　　　　(... Immediately, the mask-followers
> 　　　　fill the stage, searching for their
> 　　　　mask-bearer. Kotonu stands dazed
> 　　　　but Samson quickly raises the
> 　　　　board and pushes the mask under it.
> 　　　　It is a Driver's festival and they
> 　　　　are all armed with whips and thick
> 　　　　fibre stalks...) (Collected Plays I: 207-268).

Language in The Road, like in A Dance of the Forests becomes a major tool for the delineation of character traits. Thus, it oscillates between the carefree pidgin of Samson and Salubi to the empty bravado of Say Tokyo Kid's American slang, and the more serious language of Kotonu in his rationalizations which make him declare in a matter of fact tone the indigenous road user's pleas: "May we not walk when the road waits famished." However, the most pertinent use of language is to be found in

Professor for whom it becomes "a means of recreating and heightening an experience", according to Izevbaye (1976:54). His language becomes a central means of ritual evocation as aesthetic strategy because it often goes beyond the ordinary to its primal origin, in the process attaining ritual significance. For him, the rock and the road are two patient destroyers just like the woman lying and waiting to waste man:

> PROF: Below that bridge, a black rise of
> buttocks, two unyielding thighs and that
> red trickle like a woman washing her
> monthly pain in a thin river. So many lives
> rush in and out between her legs, and most
> of it a waste (197).

Again, to Professor, the lorry on the point of mishap is fully loaded; not with people but "pregnant with stillborns" (196) while the dead victims of an accident were "three souls" that fled up a tree and, who were "crucified on rigid branches" (159).

The songs employed in the play as noted earlier are dirge-like in content, and sung in the indigenous languages with drumming which in combination helps in eliciting fear, frenzy and orgy in the actors, and communal empathy in the audience. Thus, what emerges at the end of *The Road* is a metaphysically and sociologically significant play where both satire and tragedy interact in the ritual space. The satire expresses the cannibalistic tendencies in man which makes him find the Word elusive but opens "possibilities for a rebirth of this wounded society", to use the words of Malcolm Salt (1976:115), while the death of Professor spells the penalty for hubristic acts of daring without adequate moral will. Ritual then functions as metaphysical communication and aesthetic strategy in the play. Its form, according to Gibbs (1986:80), "is one which combines naturalism with symbolism, popular comedy with ritual, political satire with choral interludes." Similar patterns can be found in the last play under consideration.

Madmen and Specialists:

If the festival in *A Dance of the Forests* is appropriated by Forest Head for self-examination and expurgation of sins; and the celebration of Ogun's festival in *The Road* is interrupted and then aborted for personal ends by Professor, that of *Madmen and Specialists* is totally suspended. The return of Si Bero's father and Brother from the war front should have been for her an occasion for celebration. But she is brushed aside, prevented from even seeing her father, while the Old Women are uneasily waiting to see whether the family is worthy of the knowledge they have begun to impart to her. This provides the basic outline of the conflict in *Madmen and Specialists*.

Examined in the light of the concrete historical realities which gave rise to it – the Nigerian Civil war, the tragic spate of events leading to it, Soyinka's incarceration for two years, and the proliferation of sophisticated armaments all over the world – the play could then be seen as a successful blending of the particular and the universal, the metaphysical and the material historical realities through the medium of rituals. Thus, according to Obisesan (1986:159) "while objective realities are presented with palpable intensity, metaphysical corollaries are just as evident; *Madmen and Specialists* is equally apprehensible as a phenomenon encompassed within the ritual space." The overall picture emerging from the play is that of man as cannibals, a thought given vent by Soyinka as early as the time of creation of *A Dance of the Forests* and reinforced in the dispassionate Death quest of Professor and in the morally sunk community of *The Road*.

The enabling structure of *Madmen and Specialists* is a series of ritual enactments, discrete episodes which though apparently disjointed cohere ultimately in various ways to depict the myriad aberrant instincts in man. Symbolic settings, characters and situations "have been employed as distancing and universalizing devices in the play." Thus, its creative vision derives from the archetypal idioms of Obatala and Ogun which enable Soyinka to explore his metaphysical concerns of threats to continuity; the opposition forces of life and death and the creative-destructive essence seen in the symbolic characters of Bero and Old Man. The Earth Mothers – Iya Agba and Iya Mate – are, according to Obafemi (1989:11) characters derived from the traditional Ogboni cult – the force of balance in the Yoruba religious system. In the play, they register a kind of supernatural presence with one smoking a pipe and the other tending a fire. Their balancing function is performed through their store of herbs having both destructive and curative potentials.

The last set of symbolic characters comprises of the Mendicants present throughout in the backgound of the play as visible representatives of the disorder in the society. Their bodies are mangled. They could be referred to more aptly as Obatala characters as we shall establish later in the work. As the play opens, they dice off parts of their bodies mindlessly and like the layabouts of *The Road* are used in the macabre experiments of Old Man's philosophy of "As" while at the same time engaging in pungent parodies. They help complete the ritual, mysterious and unnatural atmosphere of the play.

Analysed at the level of historical reality, the prevalent situation in the unspecified setting of the play is war. A medical man, Dr. Bero, participates in the war to perform the normal functions of curing or treating those afflicted in war. However, confronted with the brutalizing effects of war, Bero metamorphoses into a brutalized and dehumanized being to give vent to this new negative awareness, Bero assumes the post of Chief Intelligence Officer of the ruling military dictatorship. Through him, we encounter Soyinka's archetypal creative-destructive duality of man's essence which is owed to Ogun. The essence is further concretized by phenomenal elements in the main setting of the play. Iya Agba in the play's opening is "smoking a thin pipe" while Iya Mate "stokes a small fire."

The fire element has been analyzed by Gibbs (1988:101-102) as symbolizing the creative-destructive principle:

> From the beginning – the two (Earth Mothers)
> are linked with fire in its multiple symbolic
> associations, its value for cooking, its ability
> to give warmth and comfort; its fearsome
> power to destroy and its being gift of
> fumigating and clearing.

Thus, instead of having metaphysical and sociological characters occupy the stage, we have characters and symbols representing facets of the attributes of the metaphysical characters. The Old Man stands as an antithesis to Bero at both the realistic and metaphysical levels. He symbolizes an opposite response to the war. The war brings out the restorative principle in him as contrasted with the destructive principle embodied in Bero. This brings to the fore, the importance of individual self-will as a theoretical component of Soyinka's philosophy. Since the war, going by the words of the Priest in his conversation with Bero, exposes everybody equally to evil:

> ... You know, it's strange how these
> disasters bring out the very best in
> man and the worst sometimes.
> In your father's case, of course, the very
> best. Truly noble (*Six Plays*, 249).

The conflicting impulses soon precipitate the inevitable clash in the play. The Old Man's activities soon bring him into conflict with the state and therefore, with his own son. First, in carrying out recuperative work among war victims, he teaches them to think. This Bero abhors:

> ... Father's assignment was to help the wounded
> re-adjust to the pieces and remnants of their bodies.
> Teach them to amuse themselves, make something
> of themselves. Instead he began to teach them to
> think, think, THINK! *Can you picture a more
> treacherous deed than to insert a working mind in a
> mangled body?* (Emphasis mine: 253).

Secondly, in his bid to drum sanity into the ears of the war commanders, forcing them to abandon the war, Old Man provides a logic illustrating war and cannibalism as correlates. He had cooked human flesh for the soldiers – without their knowing until they had eaten it. However, instead of this action eliciting aversion for cannibalistic tendencies, it only increases it. Bero himself is the first to acknowledge this: "I give you the personal word of a scientist. Human flesh is delicious. Of course, not all parts of the body. I prefer the balls myself" (*Six Plays*: 251). This is why, on discovering the ploy of the Old Man, he feels no shock or disgust because, for him, cannibalism is a way of ending inhibition.

In the father-son conflict, it is visible Soyinka's depiction of the ultimate corrupting influence of unabated power which he detests. Once on the lane of the depravity of power, Bero finds it difficult to stop. The first step is the alienation and disregard for his peers and superiors. The Earth Mothers become "stupid old hags" (246), his Big Braids "submental apes" (247) and his father "... simply another organism". The Mendicants are also symbolic of the destructive effects of power hunger which make ex-service men perpetuate the savagery of war. Their deformities are symbolic of the spiritual, moral and physical deformities of the society. They serve as dramaturgic means of presenting this situation by their parody of the dictator's moral pretensions to decency and duty. In one of the enactments of the Mendicants, the specialist is shown inflicting pain on his own father, all in the name of duty and truth. (He gives another push. Goyi screams).

> AFAA: Think not that I hurt you but that Truth hurts.
> We are all seekers after truth. I am a Specialist in truth.
> Now shall we push it up all the way, all the way?
> Or shall we have all the truth all the truth. (Another push.
> Goyi screams, then his head slumps)

After inflicting the pain, he immediately hides under the cloak of human kindness again:

> AAFAA: ... We are no monsters here. No one
>   Will charge me with heartlessness

> Give him a drink of water. A large one. Anything else?
> Perhaps you would like to use the conveniences?
> The toilet? (Goyi nods). Over there. Be my guest
> (223-224).

Such evidences of brutality proliferate in the play. And as a result of the prevalent "anomy", the Old Man becomes nihilistic and this finds expression in the philosophical abstraction called "As". "As Was, Is, Now, As Ever Shall be ..." 'As' becomes a celebration of hopelessness, for it has now become clear to Old Man that there is nothing one can do to rescue "all humanity choking in silence" (280) or stop the propping power mechanism behind barbarism supplying "As" with its favourite food which is human flesh. For, according to Oyin Ogunba (1975:203), "As seizes human reason, instigates man (through epileptic fits of religious or political fervour) to slaughter his fellow men thus providing him, (As), with his favourite dish. Just like Professor in *The Road* who has appropriately syncretized the Christian concepts of the Word as a code for his quest, Old man also subverts the Christian Ben dictum "As it was in the beginning, is now and ever shall be." Aafaa, a convert of the principle engages in an alphabetical delineation of its evil codes:

> A. Acceptance, Adjustment of Ego to the Acceptance of
> As (257).
> B, Blindness. Blindness in As... All Shall see in as
> who render themselves
> blind to all else. (257)
> C. Contentment. A full belly. (268).
> D. Divinity, Destiny is the Duty of
> Divinity. D-D-D-Destiny in 3-Dimension (257).

All these lead to the creed of the "As" doctrine: "Humanity the ultimate sacrifice to As". This important creed is susceptible to two, albeit, ominous interpretations. First, the dead victims of the aberrant regime are a part of humanity's sacrifice to "As". Secondly, the agents of the regime itself sacrifice all impulses of humanity in them. This stands out as the ultimate message of the

Old Man and is further proved by his insistent statement to Bero:

> I am the last proof of the human in you.
> The last shadow. Shadows are tough things to be rid of .
> How does one prove he was never born of man?
> Of course you could kill me...
> BERO: Or you might just die...

The Old Man's fate validates this point. As the enactments attain a ritual frenzy at the end of the play, Old Man had to be killed to snuffle out the last traces of humanity in Bero. Thus, the Old Man as tragic protagonist in an act of hubris dares the destructive cannibalistic instinct in man and pays the ultimate price. Bero acquires more power for its own sake while the Mendicants chant the nihilists' anthem. This all embracing dark vision evinced at the play's end has led Moore (1986:44-51) to describe it as one of the darkest plays of Soyinka. Jones (1973:94), on the other hand, believes that the play cannot be regarded as anything near optimistic and if there is any hope in it "is too faint".

However, in spite of the validity of these critical judgements, it is still possible to locate a note of optimism in the play. A good pointer to this is to note the seizure of the pessimistic chant of the Mendicants mid-sentence as the lights snap out. This could signify the dawn of new beginnings and to corroborate this, we find the summation of Gibbs (1985: 105-106) apt:

> Though the play is a bitter and violent attack on a sick society, the ending is not entirely without the prospect of improvement. The Old Man is dead, but the distraction caused by his death allows the Earth Mothers to destroy the herbs which the evil Bero had sought to possess. As the smoke bellows onto the stage, it is time for a new game to start but the players are different, for the Old Man is dead and Bero stands exposed as violator of the final taboos.

An attempt has been made in this chapter to establish the significance of ritual as metaphysical, communication and aesthetic strategy in Soyinka's tragic triad. Thematically, the plays explore the metaphysical concern of the playwright, in terms of the manifestation of the will of the gods in human destiny. On the level of socio-political reality, they exorcise the innate "cannibalism" in man which has led to power hunger, corruption, moral decadence and ultimately, unjustifiable bloodshed all disrupting the cosmic order. In terms of form which has been our major emphasis, the three plays are constructed on the distorted or suspended festival framework. Their internal structures consist of a series of ritual enactments, in which flashbacks play a major role in enhancing narrative fluidity, recall of past events and establishing the essential link of the continuum. Characterization is also based on the pattern of the daring Ogunnian protagonists. Demoke, Professor, Old Man – respectively acting in the midst of mediators, chorus and ritual participants.

Language in the triad performs the vital function of character identification. The role and status of the character determines his language in the ritual drama. The tragic protagonists and mediators of the ritual in some cases often take words back to their pristine roots to evoke their ritual significance. We have also established that satire in its various forms is an intrinsic dramatic component of the triad. It helps first to place the play within the realm of the contemporary. Secondly, satire serves as the tool of Soyinka's mirthless castigation of the innate cannibalistic instincts in man and lastly it enhances the essential fusion of the comic and the grave in African tragedy. A summary of our pre-occupation in this chapter could be found in the words of Osofisan (1978:163) who asserts that Soyinka's drama at its best becomes, "a symbiosis of rhetorical and ritualistic traditions, fusing essentially intellectual preoccupation with the structural machinery of rites." Next, we examine ritual as form in Soyinka's revolutionary drama.

Chapter

RITUAL AS FORM IN THE DRAMA OF LIBERATION

Our critical exploration in this chapter borders on stirring the hornet's nest, for we are lumping together three plays which differ to some extent in genre as well as artistic vision and format. In establishing a premise for our discussion in this chapter therefore, we hasten to recall that Soyinka's understanding of ritual is from a broad perspective and that a significant portion of his theory of ritual drama is dedicated to defining the relationship between ritual and revolutionary consciousness. Thus, Soyinka treats ritual as a dynamic concept which incorporates drama as a tool for the development of social consciousness. In this regard, he asserts thus:

the network (of ritual) is inextricable, the matrix of which
the ritual form is merely a shell. It is a perennial one, an
intricate evolution from tradition and history. Not merely
of myth and magic.
Ritual therefore contains its own stringent dialectic: it is
merely a visual decorative framework (Soyinka 1988:53).

Isola's revolutionary art in *Camwood on the Leaves,* Soyinka's only
published radio play is a manifestation of his commitment to
traditional values. However, both characters have in common
the urge for freedom from inhibitive forces while they seek self-
awareness, knowledge and self realization through an act of will.

The conflict in *Camwood on the Leaves*, unlike in earlier plays,
is set in a family home. The head of the family, Erinjobi, is a
reverend gentleman who has accepted the Christian religion and
thus sticks to the way of "the white man." Isola, his fifteen-year-
old son, on the other hand, would have none of the inhibitions
associated with conforming with foreign ethics. He opts radically
for a "return to the roots" by joining the Egungun cult. This
initially engenders tension at home resulting in Erinjobi's harsh
punitive measures to straighten his son:

ERINJOBI: You're a child of sorrow, do you hear?
A child of sorrow. You are lost, past redemption. I thought
this was a Christian house, but you seem determined to
turn it into a house of pagans. Don't bring shame to my
house! If I have to kill you I will see that you do not shame
my house (*Six Plays*; 117).

Ironically, this punishment merely builds a psychological
complex in Isola and worse still, strengthens his belief in the
truth of the uninhibiting traditional religion. Hence, he goes on
to commit more heinous acts regarded as abominations within
the moral code of his father's society. First, he refuses to be beaten
because he sees no justification for it:

ISOLA: I ran away too. I remember he raised the stick
against me and I took it and broke it (*Six Plays*: 107).

However, his challenge of societal convention does not end

here. He breaks the taboo of the Christian community by impregnating Morounke, the teenage daughter of Mr and Mrs Olumorin, affluent members of Reverend Erinjobi's church. For this offence and his apparent lack of a feeling of remorse, he is beaten and locked up in his father's house. He escapes and seeks refuge in his queer hiding place in the forest. It is in the forest-hut where he has been joined by the equally intimidated Morounke that the in-built psychological complex in him comes to the fore. The implications of Isola's membership of the Egungun cult also emerge. The characteristic traits of his parents have given rise to their being identified with two totemistic animals who live around his hut in the forest. The patience, love and understanding of Isola's mother makes him name the seemingly ageless tortoise Moji. The mother tortoise is believed by Isola to possess the qualities of Moji who often protects him from the wrath of his father. True to this description, when the play opens, Moji is seen pleading with her son to come out and repent because of her fear that Isola is the one that has impregnated Morounke. Moji's first words in the play are filled with a sense of desperation:

> Isola, for your mother's sake. I beg you, my son,
> open the door to me. Let me talk to you, please ... my
> son....open this door. (more desperately) Isola, what
> have I done to you? Why do you shut me out? My son,
> open the door before the wrath of God descends on
> my house (*Six Plays*: 89).

Hence, there is a psychological transference of the character and person of Moji the human, unto Moji, the tortoise as Isola strives to make Morunke realize:

> ISOLA: Have you forgotten? I gave her that name
> when we first found her.
> MOROUNKE: But that is your mother's name.
> ISOLA: She wouldn't mind. They remind me of
> each other ... they look so burdened and I cannot
> tell their age (*Six Plays*: 99-100).

Erinjobi on the other hand evokes nightmarish memories in Isola's psyche. At the same time, he has deserted the traditional religion and hence he is identified with the boa-constrictor, the symbolic representation of treachery. Ballstreri (1979:193-194) relying on the authority of Joel Adedeji's study, (1969) gives a perceptive analysis of the ritual significance of the totemic symbols used by Soyinka to represent Isola's parents. For him, the only way to understand the play and make the ending plausible is by understanding "the Yoruba belief in the magic of the conversion which takes place through the use of the masque". Thus he relates this to the Alarinjo troupe's totemistic masque of the Boa-Constrictor. He cites Adedeji:

> The most popular masque is the one that re-enacts the story of a powerful hunter who metamorphosed into a boa but owing to circumstances beyond his control could not change back to a human being. It is believed that another actor who had boasted of such metamorphic powers tried and failed to change back. Evidently, someone among the spectators had charmed him and having swooned, he had to be carried off the "circle" into a nearby bush where he was secretly resuscitated. But as far as the spectators were concerned, he had changed completely into the animal and had gone into the bush to live like the Boa for the rest of his life ("The Alarinjo Theatre": 1969:130).

The structural device of *Camwood on the Leaves* is a re-enactment of this masque. Isola named the tortoise after his mother, and the boa, after his father. To protect himself and Moji from the dangerous boa, Erinjobi, Isola keeps a loaded gun and is hurt when Morounke wastes the shot.

MOROUNKE: You shouldn't have kept it loaded.
ISOLA: I have to. There is a monster of a snake which
    lives across the stream ... over there ...in that dump of
    bamboos. It's a boa, I think ... It is a wicked snake.
    Remember the tortoise' eggs? Moji hatched them
    all and sometimes they would swim across the

stream. The snake can't swallow them so he would
pick them up and dash them to pieces against the rock
(*Six Plays*, 104).

In a series of flashbacks which at times merely look like
montage shots, Isola's endless crisis with Erinjobi which
culminates in their final confrontation and his subsequent ejection
from the house is re-enacted. The flashbacks intrude into his
consciousness as he sleeps in his hide-out in the forest with
Morounke beside him. The scenes recollected in dream sequences
from the past give him a nightmarish experience that forces him
to wake up several times moaning, shouting, and visibly shaken.
Each time, this increases Morounke's mounting anxiety until Isola
finally gives up the attempt to sleep.

> (Isola wakes up, leaps up, breathing heavily)
> MOROUNKE: Isola, what is the matter?
> ISOLA: Can't he leave me in peace?
> MOROUNKE: You were dreaming of him? Ishola,
> can't you forget him?
> ISOLA: Why doesn't he leave me alone?

Forced to abandon his sleep, he moves out into the apparently
peaceful moonlit night only to encounter the two forces haunting
his life.

> MOROUNKE: Oh, it's a full moon. Look ... there is Moji
> warming herself in the moon.
> ISOLA: She looks peaceful. Now be careful not to scare
> her off.
> MOROUNKE: Isola, look?
> ISOLA: What is it?
> MOROUNKE: By the bamboo ... there it is again
> ISOLA: Oh God it's so huge ... It's so ugly.
> ERINJOBI: I'll get him tonight ... Hurry! (126).

Isola's determination to exterminate the inhibitive force in
his life leads to his father's death as subsequent enactments show.
His rash journey home for gun powder attracts attention thus
turning him the hunter into the hunted in the hand of Erinjobi.

Mr and Mrs Olumorin and the savage stalwarts get on him. Reverend Erinjobi now is repentant and suffering from the guilt of his undue harshness on his son. He confesses, though still from the Christian viewpoint:

> ERINJOBI: What voice had I to damn you before God
> and man? My sin then became as great as yours.
> Come home and help me pray for forgiveness
> (*Six Plays*: 136).

Erinjobi, however, has registered himself as a hostile force in Isola's consciousness. And he finds it difficult to disassociate him from the python he has sworn to kill:

> ISOLA: Erinjobi, don't come in here! Go back
> to your Church and stay away. Erinjobi, stay
> away. If your head appears, Erinjobi, if your
> head appears, if your head shows once more
> between the leaves. Erinjobi! (He fires, Morounke
> screams, begins to cry. Approaching footsteps running)
> (*Six Plays:* 138.

Thus, Isola murders his father, psychologically satisfied that he has ended the terror of the boa in the forest. However, the action is plausible as remarked earlier on if we consider Balistreri's view point: "Isola is not crazy, and he does not believe that a snake can talk; he does believe in the magic of the masque, since he is a member of the Egungun cult, and he does believe that his father is transformed into the boa" ('1979:94). Whatever the case may be, the essence of Isola's daring act is two-fold. First, Erinjobi's death becomes a ritual sacrifice of expiation for the community and his transgressions against the ancestors. Secondly, and perhaps most importantly, his death in spite of its tragic consequences has liberated Isola from the clutches of an alien system which grants special privileges to the likes of Mr and Mrs Olumorin as wealthy members of the Church and which denies him access to the knowledge of truth and self-awareness which he could not locate in the father's religion. *Camwood on the Leaves,* as a radio play requires a structural device for smooth transition from one scene to the other, especially because it has a proliferation of flashbacks which helps to link the past with the present. Songs are used by Soyinka to achieve this and to further emphasize the awareness that the scenes are far from being chronological presentations. However, the choral chants also perform the other essential function of commenting on the dramatic action in the play and of helping to set the mood for the scenes. Within this perspective, the ritual dirge with which the play opens and ends provides a clue to its overall vision:

> Mourning her child, agbe wrapped herself in indigo
> mourning her child, aluko ground the Camwood dye. The
> bereaved father forged bells of brass but we cannot dwell
> too much on these things. Lest we are caught in a fatal
> game with the gods ... (*Six Plays*: 139).

The other two plays we shall be dealing with in the rest of this chapter are based on communal festivities channelled to foster communal liberation.

Kongi's Harvest: A recurrent feature of the contemporary African political scene is the advent of leaders who, having tasted power, find it difficult relinquishing it, and hence degenerate into despots and dictators, inventing repressive stratagems to perpetuate themselves in power. The artist, being a sensitive member of the society, and more often than not the main butt of such dictatorial governments seeks ways of detracting from the pretended glamour of the dictators or of advocating outright collective confrontation of such opprobrious powers. Soyinka's *Kongi's Harvest* is a combination of the two artistic approaches, a satirical portrayal of the newly emerged dictator culminating into a charged climax of confrontation between the dictator and the state institutions on the one hand and the collective force of the people on the other.

Like several of the major plays already discussed and as its title proclaims, the dramatic context of this play is one of celebration. Precisely, the harvest ceremony is one in which the

Oba, both as spiritual and political head, ushers in the New Year and the harvest season by publicly eating amidst pomp and panoply a specially selected yam, harvested in the season. Ogunba (1970:8) has placed the context of the play in correct perspective:

> In **Kongi's Harvest,** the design is that of a King's festival, especially a Yoruba King's festival. The king in Africa is still God's deputy on earth and so he combines both spiritual and political functions. Hence, this festival is not a private celebration but one that has meaning for the whole community and in which everyone is expected to participate with interest. As the first citizen, the ideal figure around whom the whole tradition is woven, the king's dance is the dance of the community by its divine leader, a re-enactment of the whole living tradition of the people. It is thus a life-giving ritual which has to be done in epic style to demonstrate the higher aspirations of the community.

However, the post-independence socio-political reality in Africa is that of a distorted, abused and usurped life-sucking ritual by the tyrannical dispensation of Kongi. He seeks to annihilate the old order because of its supposed backwardness and obfuscation, and therefore the blocking of the path to progress. Thus, when the play opens, the authentic spiritual father of the land is held captive in a detention camp. As dramatic action commences with a roll of drums and the subsequent rendition of the special anthem by the retinue of the traditional rulers led by the deposed Oba Danlola himself, what traditionally is a pre-sacrifice invocatory chant to the founder and royal ancestors of the community rendered in rich praise poetry now becomes at once a song of submission to the military might of the dictatorship and a satirization of the barrenness of its all pervading propaganda machinery fostered on meaningless "isms":

> Who says there isn't plenty word in a penny
> Newspaper ... who but a lunatic will bandy words
> with boxes. With government rediffusion sets which
> talk and talk and never take one word in reply

(Collected Plays 2:62).

Kongi having usurped and consolidated the political leadership of Ismaland, remains haunted by the need for spiritual control which still resides with Oba Danlola even in his denigrated state in prison; hence, Kongi's ingeneous determination to publicly hijack spiritual leadership from the Oba during the festival of the New Year by forcing the presentation of the symbolic yam to him which will signify the ultimate submission of Oba Danlola to the political and spiritual might of the new autocrat. The context is also symbolic of the collapse of traditional ethos and the entrenchment of vulgar modernism. The major conflict in *Kongi's Harvest* emerges through the process of persuasion, coercion and myriad tactics of Kongi through his state dogs, and the age old cunning of a traditional ruler who is being cajoled into committing political suicide, and the anger of a youthful successor set to confront both with all its tragic and comic manifestations. Heywood (1976:47-48) therefore captures succinctly the dramatic conflict of *Kongi's Harvest*:

> The play shows that there is little to choose between the two autocrats who have everything in common except style and the weight of tradition. Danlola is moribund; Kongi is a killer: Daodu is life, Kongi harvests death: Daodu with his farmer's commune harvests life. He is Danlola's rightful successor but he is with the common people too. He challenges Kongi, not as the pretender but as a revolutionary leader.

From the above, three forces can be seen to have emerged from this play of political intrigues. First is the Oba with his royal appendages. Second is the autocratic Kongi and his subjugated and subjugating institutions like the Organizing Secretary, the Aweris and the Carpenter's Brigade. Lastly, the third group comprises of Daodu, Danlola's heir-apparent; Segi, Kongi's former mistress and daughter of one of the condemned acolytes of Danlola and the masses who constitute the farm commune. Of the three groups, only the last is spared the power of Soyinka's excoriation through which he exposes the corruption, deception and immorality of mainly the second group and to some extent the first which runs through the play.

The play opens as said earlier with a prologue entitled "Hemlock" which finds the spiritual ruler of Ismaland imprisoned in a detention camp intoning a satirical tune. The foreboding of this opening develops into a bold stamp of the prevalent cosmic distortion and decadence as Oba Danlola is subjected to degrading confrontations with minions like the Prison Superintendent and the Organizing Secretary. This further deepens the crisis especially with the Superintendent's stoppage of the royal drums leading to the exchange of invectives and the threat of malediction hanging on the person of the Superintendent. The tragic depth of the prevalent anomaly is finally established through the scenes concluding the dance of mourning:

> ... the drums are newly shaped and stiff arms strain on stubborn crooks, so delve with the left foot for ill luck; once more with left alone, for disaster is the only certainty we know... (69).

The play proper, starting from the "First Part" is a series of enactments which open on the caricature of the institution which has supplanted the traditional system mourned in "Hemlock". President Kongi has retreated to the mountains for pre-festival fasting and meditation. To "dispute" the subjects of his meditation and strengthen him in his task, the members of the Reformed Aweri Fraternity are forced into the retreat of meditation in starvation. The picture is rendered complete with the stationing of "The Carpenter's Brigade", the indoctrinated youth arm of the regime to serve the dual purpose of mouthing the praise of Kongi and providing at the same time security against potential insurgents.

However, the entire set-up just like other things associated with the regime is fake, superficial and pretentious. The Reformed Aweri known for conducting sleeping sessions engage in petty squabbles or engage in bribe-yielding ventures. Their notion of a public image and pronouncement to replace the traditional advisory council is built around a wall of statistical nonsense:

> ... Only ideograms in algebraic quantums, if the square of XQX (2bc) equals QA into the square root of X, then the progressive forces must prevail over the reactionary in the span of .32 of a single generation (*Collected Plays*, 172).

Kongi himself while in retreat does not object to an intruding photographer for whom he strikes poses to be accompanied with the meaningless appellations thought up by his self-seeking Secretary:

> A leader's Temptation ... Agony on the Mountains
> the loneliness of the pure ... the uneasy Head ... a saint
> at Twilight ... the spirit of the Harvest ... the face of
> Benevolence ... The Giver ... (93).

The main segment of the alternating enactments of the "First Part" could however be found in activities taking place in the pub operated by Daodu and Segi. The night-club, apart from serving as a social resort, is also a rallying point for the opposing progressive movement, coordinated by Daodu and Segi. The scene finds Kongi's Organizing Secretary intruding into the terrain of the arch opponents of the government to plead for the intercession of Daodu in the stalemate engendered by Oba Danlola's refusal to abdicate spiritual leadership to Kongi by agreeing to hand him the New Year Yam on the festival day. Desperation forces him to initiate concessions on behalf of Kongi, to the effect of releasing the four political prisoners as a last minute gesture of magnanimity by the government. Daodu eventually agrees after a lot of verbal exchanges between him and the Secretary which expose the weaknesses and paranoia of the dictatorial regime.

This "First Part" thrives on flashbacks which enable Soyinka to supply answers to questions which would have hitherto arisen.

The main enactment is the night-club encounter. This is constantly interrupted by the juxtaposition of scenes showing the four sessions held by the Secretary with the President to gain concession for his present bargaining at the club. However, an additional scene which more appropriately bears description as a flash forward upsets the achievements of the Organizing Secretary and the source of joy mounting in Segi's club. The location is Kongi's retreat and the Secretary is hard-pressed, facing the wrath of Kongi at the latest news of the escape of one of the prisoners and the suicide of another. The development maddens Kongi who immediately suspends the reprieve and works himself into an epileptic fit which ends the first part in suspense as the tableau shows.

> (His mouth hanging open, from gasps into spasms and
> violent convulsions, Kongi goes into an epileptic fit.
> Over his struggle for breath rises Kongi's chant.) (*Collected
> Plays II,* 100).

The "Second Part" opens on the festival day itself with a myriad of bustling festival activities. Oba Danlola, released just in time to make preparation for the festival, is seen at the height of his obviously deceptive "preparation". He is enmeshed in his cunning antics "trying out one thing, rejecting it and trying on another" to the discomfiture of Dende, and more importantly Daodu, who increasingly gets alarmed at the pace of the Oba's preparation. If Danlola initially agrees to yield (this is doubtful), Kongi's sudden change of stance immediately re-affirms his refusal to participate in the act of final humiliation. Yet, without giving voice to this, he still manipulates his troubled heir-apparent:

> DAODU: I thought we agreed on that and
> you gave your word ....
> DANLOLA: You should, my son, when you
> deal in politics, pay sharp attention to the
> word. I agreed only that I would prepare myself for the
> grand ceremony, not that I would go (*Collected Plays II:*
> 102-103).

Daodu's onerous task becomes impossible with the arrival of the junior king, Sarumi, amidst a performing orchestra which immediately transforms the palace into a festival arena. The revolutionary ploy of Daodu and Segi with their followers appears to be heading for jeopardy and in desperation Daodu commits the second major abomination of the play against tradition by puncturing the lead drum:

> DANLOLA: Life gets more final everyday.
> That prison Superintendent merely lays his hands
> on my lead drummer and stopped the singing, but
> you, our son and heir, you've seen to the song itself (111).

The magnitude of the desecration and the ensuing consternation forces Daodu to yield his ultimate secret. Segi who stands the loss of her father and in solidarity with whom Danlola is apparently boycotting the festival is anxious that it goes on undisrupted for undisclosed but strategic reasons. Danlola is finally appeased and heads for the grounds:

> It seems our son will make us mere
> spectators at our own feast....
> Well, I will not bear the offering
> Past the entrance to the mosque
> Only a phony drapes himself in
> deeper indigo than the son of
> the deceased (114-115).

From then on, the flourish of activities is transferred to the festival ground with the Secretary somewhere buried in a last minute supervision of entrances and the decoration of festival arenas. However, three incidents are vital to the core of our analysis and the eventual climax of the play. First, the Women's Auxiliary Corps unexpectedly led by Segi overshadows the government's Carpenter's Brigade. They storm the arena triumphantly carrying Daodu whose communally harvested yam has won the New Yam Competition. Secondly, we have Daodu's unhidden subversive speech castigating the regime of terror made inside the protective cordon of oppressed generality which betrays his revolutionary intents but whose effects are lost on President Kongi.

Thirdly, as Kongi finishes the speech a "burst of gun-fire which paralyses everyone" (128) is heard from off-stage. This brings the impending confrontation of the opposing camps to a head as the Secretary reports the death of Segi's father to a satisfied Kongi and later to an unruffled Segi who declares:

> Yes, let it all end tonight. I am tired
> of being the mouse in his cat- and mouse
> game.

Inspired by the seeming victory of the moment, Kongi launches into a tirade of speeches deriding "the enemies of state." The speech is reminiscent of the typical political address of African leaders against real or imagined enemies, full of invectives but barren of cogent policy statements:

> The spirit of Harvest has smitten the enemies
> of Kongi. The justice of earth has prevailed over traitors
> and conspirators. There is divine blessing on the second
> five-year Development Plan. The spirit of resurgence is
> cleansed in the blood of the nations' enemies (129-130).

Unknown to him, the celebration is to end on a maledictory note. In a decisive move symbolic of the ultimate confrontation of the revolutionary forces with the repressive regime, Segi, after a brief exit, returns with Kongi's harvest.

> (A copper salver is raised suddenly high. It passes from
> hand to hand above the women's heads; they dance with
> it on their heads; it is thrown from one to the other until
> at last it reaches Kongi's table and Segi throws open the
> lid. In it, the head of an old man) (131-132).

In the ensuing melee which leaves Kongi with the head in "speechless terror", the play proper ends on a note of anarchy symbolizing the visibly shaken administration of Kongi. Echoes of the aftermath of the aborted festival could be gleaned from the "Hangover," a sort of epilogue to the play. The Organizing

Secretary and Oba Danlola, both prominent actors of the new dictatorship and the old traditional autocracy respectively, are engaged in a frantic bid to escape to the border, apparently towards self-exile. Their meeting allows a final exchange of insults revealing further that the difference between the two governments is not much. Perhaps, the most significant news of the epilogue is the report of Danlola on the ploy to abduct the revolutionary duo of Daodu and Segi. There are strong indications that they may resist the "forcible abduction" and elect to carry through the fight already started with Kongi. In the meantime anarchy reigns.

Apart from *Death and the King's Horseman, Kongi's Harvest* remains the only major play in which Soyinka makes use of the total resources of language and music at various levels: ritual, revolutionary and satirical. The play's opening anthem is an admixture of ritual evocation and satire. We have earlier on drawn out the satiric elements of the "Hemlock" hence we now examine its ritual content. The anthem is in a way a summation of the tragic dimensions of Kongi's reign and the death of the traditional institution with its life-giving potentials.

> The pot that will eat fat
> Its bottom must be scorched
> The squirrel that will long crack nuts
> Its foot pad must be sore ...(61).

The two Yoruba proverbs poetically linked have been perceptively interpreted by Jones (1977, 73) as signifying two thematic implications for the play. First is its reference to what Oyin Ogunba (1970:4) describes as the "self imposed herculean assignment" of Kongi, Second is the equally hard task of unseating him which Daodu and Segi are engaged in. Both ways, no reference is made to the traditional order whose atrophy is imminent as dramatized in the "ege" funeral dirge which is accompanied by the "gbedu" cultic drum:

SARUMI: They complained because the first
        of the new yams

>Melted first in an Oba's mouth.
>But the dead will witness
>We drew poison from the root (66).

Oba Sarumi's mournful monotone in reply to the drummer, draws attention to the spiritual essence of the King's duty of tasting the new yam as a means of averting cosmic disruption, or epidemic and ensure communal stability. It is this responsibility that Kongi seeks to usurp and this results in grave anomally:

> DRUMMER: I saw a strange sight in the market this day,
> The day of the feast of Agemo...
> OGBO AWERI: This is the last that we shall dance together,
> This is the last the hairs
> Will lift on our skin
> And draw together
> When the gbedu rouses
> The dead in Osugbo (67).

The Agemo is the spirit of a cult usually responsible for maintaining justice in the society. Its sudden appearance in the market-place, the rallying point of the community, is disturbing. The dislocation which it signals is further complicated by the Osugbo's (Council of Elders) rousing of the dead who are supposed to be guardians of the cosmic realm. The culmination of this anomaly could only engender disruption as the monster child President Kongi is born:

> OGBO AWERI: Observe when the monster child was born,
> Opele taught us to
> Abandon him beneath the buttress tree
> But the mother in us said, oh no,
> A child is still a child ...(68).

The consequences of this indulgence are grave as seen in the reply of Sarumi which follows. In the same vein, Ismaland's indulgence in not curbing the excesses of Kongi has made him grow into an uncontrollable conqueror of all, including the spiritual institutions of the land. Elements of Yoruba ritual poetry, music, mime and dance proliferate in the play. However, from this early stage in the play no pretensions are made that the traditional order is set for a fight with the "monster" regime. The real fight lies between it and the revolutionary forces of Daodu and Segi.

To justify this conclusion, we have to take a look at Daodu's fiery language. In a moment of naked realization of the opposition of his life-giving role as spirit of harvest to the life inhibiting governance of Kongi, he pleads to be allowed to play his role through physical action. In spite of Segi's plea that only life and love is worth preaching, Daodu cannot be restrained from pouring his "imprecations" and "curses":

> On all who fashion chains, on farmers of
> Terror, on builders of walls, on all who
> Guard against the night but breed darkness by day
> On all whose feet are heavy and yet stand upon the
> world...
> On all who see not with eyes of the dead?
> But with eyes of Death ... (*Collected Plays* 1:99).

The proof of Daodu's revolutionary zeal is evident in the subversive activities of the farm community which he coordinates and his fearless denunciation of Kongi's regime at the festival. The songs of Segi's Women Corps are also overtly subversive:

> ... A burden of logs
> Climbed the hunch back frill
> There was no dearth of yam
> But the head of the first born
> Was pounded for yam
> There was no dearth of wood
> Yet the thigh of the first born
> Lost its bone for fuel (141).

In rounding off our discussion of *Kongi's Harvest*, it is essential to note a trend in the plays treated so far. This is Soyinka's conscious attempt to place the motivations for, and resolutions of, human conflict in the hands of human characters. He thus proves our assertion that ritual in its various manifestations essentially serves as a framework for dramatizing the liberation of human consciousness. The gods are referred to, the ritual cults invoked, the characters share traits with the gods but dramatic actions and reactions are activated by the human factor. A similar attempt to hold human beings responsible for their fate is discernible in *The Bacchae of Euripides,* Soyinka's adaptation whose original emphasized the influence of the gods in human affairs.

A starting point for the discussion of Soyinka's artistic intent "to appropriate ritual for ideological statements" in *The Bacchae of Euripides* is the examination of his note of protest to the key figures of the 1973 premiere of the play:

> I regard this play as an "extravagant banquet", an expression of the periodic human need to swill, gorge and copulate on the same gargantuan scale as Nature herself. It seems to me that there is a reluctance to accept this definition.

Soyinka retains most of the outlines of the story of Euripides's original play. But in order to achieve what Jones (1983:114) describes as his more important factor of attraction to the play which "was the opportunity it gave him to look once again, in this removed context, at the theme of government and its attendant themes of justice and freedom," he at once makes a number of significant departures from the original. The first in this direction is the militaristic portrayal of Pentheus. Adebayo Williams (1980:91) made a note of this: "Soyinka's version of Pentheus is more severe, more ruthless, more autocratic and impatient of criticism than Euripides's. In his sauciness and ill-tempered contempt for all democratic procedure, he reminds one of a latter day version of King Kongi".

Like Kongi, he is an autocrat with a penchant for words of command. Hence, his first speech in the play upon his return from the journey is intimidating:

> I shall have order! Let the city
> Know at once Pentheus is here to give
> Back order and sanity ...

He then goes ahead to set armed agents on the celebrating Bacchantes without bothering to consider any statements of explanation:

> ... Ino and Automao
> My own mother
> Agave are principals at the obscenities!
> I'll teach them myself. I have woven
> Iron nets to trap them. I'll bring an
> End to the cunning subversion ... (*The Bacchae*, 27-28).

This fierce militarism is equally corroborated by the opening tableau which gives the audience an insight into Pentheus's kingdom.

> To one side, a road dips steeply into lower
> background, lined by the bodies of crucified
> slaves mostly in the skeletal stage (*The Bacchae*, 1).

To provide a counteracting force against Pentheus' regime in line with his intentions, Soyinka also creates a voice for the slaves whose head, the Slave Leader serves as a mobilizing agent for the oppressed members of the Greek class society. He is bent on leading the slaves in rebellion against the unjust system and reinforces this with the support of Dionysos:

> You hesitant fools!
> Don't you understand?
> Don't you know?
> We are no longer alone Slaves,...
> This master race, this much vaunted dragon spawn
> Have met their match.
> Nature has joined forces with us.
> (*The Bacchae of Euripides*, 7).

The Slave Leader forcefully argues for a stoppage of the yearly ritual sacrifice of slaves during the Eleusis festival, saying that the class which benefits from it should elect from within it the festival scapegoat:

> SLAVE LEADER: Why us? Why always us,
> HERDSMAN: Why not?
> SLAVE LEADER: Because the rites bring us nothing!
> Let those to whom the profits go bear the burden of the
> old year dying (4).

The structural device through which Soyinka develops both the theme of class conflict and the required atmosphere of harvest and orgy of the humans and the gods is ritualism which functions as an aesthetic and communicational strategy through song, dance, mime and mask. Soyinka uses song in his version of *The Bacchae* to create a scene of religious ecstasy at the moment in the play when the Bacchantes and the slaves who have hitherto secretly worshipped Dionysos, join forces and openly worship their god. The resultant possession as described by Soyinka is similar to the ritual masques of Yoruba traditional festivals and the dance of possession described by de Graft which we cited in the first chapter:

> The scene which follows needs the following quality: extracting the emotional colour and temperature of a European pop scene without degenerating into that tawdry commercial manipulation of teenage mindlessness. The lines are chanted not sung, to musical accompaniments. The slave leader is not a gyrating pop drip. His control emanates from the self-contained force of his person, a progressively deepening spiritual presence. His style is based on the lilt and energy of the black hot gospellers who themselves are often first to become physically possessed. The effect on his crowd is, however, the same-physically as would be seen in a teenage pop audience. From orgasmic means the surrogate climax is achieved, A scream finds its electric response in others and a rush begins for the person of the preacher ... (*The Bacchae of Euripides*, 18).

The most significant mime in the play is that of sacrifice which comes immediately after the "two wedding feasts", a mime which reminds one of the concept of communion. But the communal worship about to commence cannot take place without prior sacrifice. Thus, the sacrifice is mimed as the Bacchantes and the slaves are joined in worship with a series of invocative speeches by their leaders whose end culminates in "a stylized mime of the hunt" (*The Bacchae of Euripedes*: 80). This mime foreshadows the ultimate sacrifice of Pentheus.

However, it is through the medium of dance that other important events and the resolution of the play take place. Dionysos uses dance to arouse possession and religious ecstasy to bring about the seeming cannibalistic action of the women which enable him carry through his vengeance against Pentheus – the despot. Two stage notes describe this scene vividly:

> (Agave runs in with her trophy struck on a thyrsus
> but invisible under gold ribbons. She raises the stave
> and the ribbons flow around her as she runs once more
> round the stage)
> (She takes the thyrsus in both hands and
> whirls it. The Maenads chase and catch the ribbons
> as they unfurl and float outwards. With Agave in the
> centre, a Maypole dance evolves naturally from their
> positions. It is a soft graceful dance).
> (*The Bacchae*: 87-90).

Thus, the community saw to the end of a dictator at the climax of their harvest festival. Apparently, this event could otherwise have made the play a tragedy as in the original but the playwright introduces an ingeneous ending which turns and portrays the tragic end of Pentheus as "a restorative act, a necessary communal sacrifice which will bring into being a new kind of society." (Stratton 1988:548). This is the substance of Teiresias' consolation to Kadmos, the mourning grandfather of Pentheus:

> O, Kadmos, it was a cause beyond madness this scattering
> of his flesh to the seven winds, the rain of blood that

streamed but endlessly to soak our land (97).

The final transformation of the blood-spurting head of Pentheus to a fountain of wine from which the community, both slave and master, sip gives the play its desired end of a harvest that leads into change and liberation. Thus, through a combination of ritual components, the use of metaphysical beings like Dionysos whom the artist successfully links with Ogun (a background prepared earlier on in "The Fourth Stage,") and ritual aesthetics like song, dance, mime and mask, Soyinka is able to carve out an essentially African communal drama of universal relevance, using a borrowed classical myth.

We have striven thus far to establish the overt or covert use of ritual as framework in Soyinka's plays which essentially deal with contemporary issues of liberation. We have elucidated with textual materials the varying presence of ritual as mainly communication and aesthetic strategies while de-emphasizing the metaphysical concerns as essences. Through our explications in the previous chapters and the present one, we have studied extensively the myriad manifestations of ritual as form and content in the entire dramatic oeuvre of the playwright under examination. Hence, on the strength of the emerging data, we could validate our critical assumption at the beginning of this work, correlates of which can be found in the assertion of Adelugba (1987:177) that in Soyinka's plays, there are; "Rituals of Rebellion, of Purification, of Exorcism, of Worship and indeed of Celebration." Next, we turn our attention to the identification and exemplification of the technical and aesthetic constants of this ritual dramaturgy.

Chapter

5

❧

TECHNICAL AND AESTHETIC CONSTANTS OF RITUAL DRAMA

Our preoccupation thus far has been with the textual elucidation of the formal and thematic continuum in Soyinka's use of ritual as metaphysical, communication and aesthetic strategy in his dramatic works. However, whether on the transcendental plane of the communal search for self-rejuvenation through transition, or exorcision of human excrescences culminating in the returning cycle or appropriating ritual for its liberative potentials; certain architectonic elements recur as dramaturgic imperatives in the works of Soyinka.

The intention in this chapter is to collate these dramaturgic elements as a stepping stone to a critical evaluation of the playwright's dramatic ensemble. The first major recurrent dramaturgic element is the concept of archetypal characterization. Two character types are discernible in the works of Soyinka: the metaphysical and the sociological. Metaphysical characters comprise of gods chosen from the Yoruba pantheon to explicate his worldview. They also include spirits and myriad phenomenal forces lying guardian to the gulf of transition whose operational existence is psychologically reckoned with in plays where they do not take bodily forms as is the case in *A Dance of the Forests*.

The chosen gods as noted before now are Obatala, Ogun and Esu. Where these gods are physically present, they take on imagistic representations in human form, exhibiting the virtues and foibles of the latter as seen in *A Dance of the Forests* where we have Ogun, Esuoro and Obatala masquerading as Obaneji and Forest Head respectively. In *The Bacchae of Euripides*, Dionysos, whose correlation with Ogun is consciously foregrounded, appears physically to establish his worship and take side with the commoners in liquidating the oppressive rule of Pentheus. In the major plays where the gods are not present, they manifest themselves through human surrogates, serving either as functional representatives or as aesthetic symbols.

Soyinka employs the Obatala archetypes mainly as heroes in his plays. This will not be surprising if we bear in mind Obatala's character traits which, as outlined above, include patience, suffering and self-sacrifice on behalf of the community. We referred earlier to the Obatala and Sango myth, demonstrating these attributes which is essentially a tale of captivity, suffering and release. In this respect, Forest Head the central mediator of the rites of passage at the Gathering of the Tribes, the blind Beggar from Bukanji and Teiresias "the poor agent of the gods" who hopes to restore meaning to the Eleusis festival and prevent a slave uprising by offering himself as a scapegoat are all Obatala characters in *A Dance of the Forests, The Swamp Dwellers* and *The Bacchae of Euripides* respectively. Apart from these, a number of other deformed symbolic characters also people Soyinka's plays. These are directly traceable to, and can aptly be described as,

"Obatala's children" to use the words of Balistreri (1979: 113). They are the products of that moment of mistake when Obatala fell for the ploy of Esu. To atone for this error, Obatala is often close to these characters, imbuing them with the power of foresight in spite of their suffering; and, atimes, endowing them with some of his attributes. There are manifestations of Obatala's children in the important roles played by Ifada and Girl in *The Strong Breed,* Aroni the special assistant of Forest Head and the Half-Child symbolic representation of Nigeria's future in *A Dance of the Forests.* Murano, trapped in the state of transition and held captive by Professor in *The Road,* as well as the Mendicants in *Madmen and Specialists* also fall into the category of Obatala's children. All these characters are further traceable to Obatala because they are not responsible for their conditions but are either naturally afflicted or deformed through people seeking to acquire power or other benefits.

The Obatala characters are an epitome of the human ability to persevere since they witness the suffering of humanity but do not possess the ability to stop them. Obatala's children are themselves chips off Obatala characters. They possess insights into the human condition bearing the suffering of mankind, patiently and atimes symbolizing this patience. The quiet nature of these characters generates very low dramatic potential; a reason why they are often paired with more active characters. Though these active characters may also suffer and sacrifice, they do so as a matter of conscious choice and creative expression of individual will. These are the Ogun characters.

Soyinka's central dramatic personae in his major plays are the tragic protagonists who, as said earlier on in Chapter One, are modelled after Ogun, the god of destruction and creativity. Apart from the god's imagistic appearance in *A Dance of the Forests* and *The Bacchae of Euripides*, Demoke, Igwezu, Eman, Isola, Daodu, Olunde, Professor and the Slave Leader all emerge as Ogun characters possessing the daring attributes of the god in varying proportions in the plays analysed thus far. Unlike Obatala characters, the Ogun characters are strong individuals having links with Ogun either through their profession or other character traits. They possess a fair share of the excesses and challenging nature of the Ogunnian personality, a reason why they usually challenge other men, the community's traditional values and beliefs and atimes representatives of the gods through their strength of will. However, as with Ogun's primal tragic act, these daring acts do not often go unpunished because they usually upset the natural balance which requires a confrontation or a journey through the abyss of transition and an act of sacrifice for the restoration of order. However, through their actions, the human community often gains self-awareness, regeneration or liberation as shown in our various analyses of the plays featuring the characters. These tragic protagonists have the greatest potential for engendering or sustaining dramatic conflict hence Soyinka has consistently featured them in his tragedies and other major plays.

Finally, in terms of archetypal characterization, Soyinka creates Esu characters modelled after the deity who is the god of chance and destiny, in addition to being a wily trickster. Apart from his artful nature which often places him as an antagonist to other gods and people's aspirations, Soyinka is also attracted to Ogun for his potentials for engendering chaos, humour and satire in his works. Examples of these characters are Esuoro and Danlola in *A Dance of the Forests*, and *Kongi's Harvest*, respectively. Esuoro is the combination of two gods, Esu is the trickster "full of machinations" and Oro is both a god and the agent of the Yoruba death cult. Apart from his consistent effort to bring Demoke to book for killing Oremole and the sacrilege on his tree, Esu is also determined to thwart the case of the humans before Forest Father. Aroni becomes suspicious of the cruel and accusing Questioner of the Dead Woman and the Dead Man from the past in part two of the play only to discover it was Esuoro. The stage instruction describing this goes thus.

(Aroni reaches out suddenly and rips off the Questioner's
mask.
It is Esuoro, and he immediately rushes off)
(*Collected Plays 1*:63).

Despite Forest Head's warning to the interpreter in the play,
he is discovered to be Esuoro's jester who, together with Esuoro
himself, disguising as the figure in red have temporarily succeeded
in winning the control of mankind's future symbolized in the
Half-Child. Ogun had to engage in combat with him to rescue
the Half-Child from the wiles of Esuoro. The manifestations of
the Esu character in Oba Danlola are visible through his various
antics of undermining the encroaching dictatorial military might
of Kongi, Though, the institution he represents lacked the power
to fight Kongi's regime, he thwarts through cunning machinations
the determined wish of spiritual usurpation by Kongi.

The presence of these gods and other metaphysical beings
or their surrogates apart from their dramatic potentials serve to
portray Soyinka's concept of the cyclic continuum of the living,
the dead and the unborn. Secondly, they help dramatize the
notion of the primal eruption of cosmic harmony which has
necessitated the annual rites of sacrifice to stem the eruptions;
or propitiate the forces responsible for it. Thirdly, by imbuing
the gods with strengths and weaknesses like human beings,
Soyinka seeks to engender self-awareness, pointing out that both
the fallibility of the gods and the human potent cosmic disruption,
an end to which must always be sought outside the caprices of
the gods.

Apart from the archetypal characters, Soyinka's drama also
features a number of elements borrowed and adapted from the
traditional animist festivals. These are the mediators and the
chorus in the ritual drama. After the tragic protagonists or atimes
scapegoats, the mediators become the next most important
characters since they direct affairs in the ritual arena and ensure
a smooth transition or closure of the ritual proceedings.
According to Hepburn (1988:585) who we are citing for the
second time "mediators of ritual closure are straight, even harsh,

characters for good reason: They concern themselves with the world as they know it, and they attempt to keep that world in place". This definition appears like a description of the role of mediators in traditional rituals which she must have had in mind, but Soyinka is a contemporary artist dealing with contemporary issues. Mediators for him become a part of the entire apparatus for realizing his differing intentions of transition, exorcism or stirring rebellion, a reason why they come in varied forms.

Perhaps of all of Soyinka's mediators, only Iyaloja and to some extent, Jaguna and Oroge fit Hepburn's definition. These mediators are responsible for directing rituals involving human sacrifice as a means of strengthening and regenerating their communities as well as ensuring continuity. In situations where tragic protagonists seek to endanger the goals of renewal by non-cooperation, the mediators have to intervene to ensure the completion of such rituals as shown in the two plays where these characters feature respectively. However, as shown earlier on in our analysis, only Iyaloja in *Death and the King's Horseman* displays the moral strength necessary for carrying such responsibilies through. Jaguna and Oroge have been shown to compromise taboos in the ritual process thus betraying their loss of faith in such rituals which merely pre-empts the community's questioning of the moral justification of the whole process. Other mediators are simply corrupt, and they appropriate ritual for their own selfish ends, thus becoming discredited. The Organizing Secretary in *Kongi's Harvest* who mediates between the opposing forces in order to ensure a successful New Yam celebration becomes corrupt, amassing wealth for his own ends. He is forced into exile as the ritual he mediates ends in disaster.

However, other mediating characters fail, not because of corruption, but because they simply lose control of the ritual procedure and are thus forced to contend with the sad outcome of their endeavours. Morounke in *Camwood on the Leaves,* in spite of her passionate efforts, cannot prevent the tragic end of the conflict between her husband and his parents. Samson's mediation in *The Road* is directed toward ensuring his survival and that of Kotonu, and also on the proper conduct of affairs in Professor's shack. He is at the centre of most of the enactments in the play but could not control the violence that bursts out in the end. Si Bero in *Madmen and Specialists* suffers a similar fate. Lastly, there are self-sacrificing mediators who operate with the power of hindsight which enables them to foretell or pre-empt the end of the ritual procedures. Examples are Forest Head who co-ordinates the aborted celebration of the Gathering of the Tribes, linking the worlds of the continuum in the chthonic realm to bring the humans to self-confession and expiation and Teiresias the prophetic seer in *The Bacchae of Euripides*. But irrespective of the nature of their mediation, these mediating characters only lead a group of participants or communicants in the ritual drama who are responsible for enacting the incidents of the ritual procedures.

Our analysis here has benefited from the insights provided by Osofisan (1978:528) who has described the chorus as one of the multiplicity of devices through which Soyinka increases the impact both of the satire and the tragic awareness in his plays. However, we disagree with him on matters of details. As stressed in our first chapter, the traditional ritual drama is made up of the tragic protagonist, the mediator or Chief Priest, and the participants who form the chorus. Together, they re-enact the past, invoke the gods, dance and sing until a final cathartic moment is reached which is mainly psychical and collective. Ropo Sekoni (1987:84) describes the process in the following way:

> Like drama, ritual usually involves the playing
> of roles, the presence of an audience, the
> evolution of events from an initial position of conflict
> to a terminal point of resolution.

To elicit the same communal participation both at the emotional and intellectual levels in modern ritual drama, Soyinka has devised a means of transferring past enactments and psychological experiences to visible stage actions. This he does by making selected actors among the participants act out incidents which belong to the past, the present, and even the future as they are recollected. These enactments illustrate our concept of ritual as communication strategy and constitute the core of Soyinka's plays as shown by our textual explications. They are achieved through a number of techniques already illustrated in our previous analysis and which we shall soon come to examine again.

The number of chorus characters working with the Mediator varies from play to play. In *A Dance of the Forests*, there are Rola, the prostitute; Demoke, the sculptor; and Adenebi, the Council Orator. With Samson, the mediator in *The Road,* are Salubi, Kotonu, Say Tokyo Kid and Murano. *Madmen and Specialists* has the four Medicants led by the Aafaa. In *The Strong Breed* are characters from Eman's past like Old Man, his father; Omae his bethrothed; and then the Priest. In *Death and the King's Horseman* we have Amusa, Praise Singer, the school girls, market women and so on. The chorus forms an integral part of Soyinka's ritual drama for it performs a number of functions in conjunction with the mediator, which ensures fluidity in the unfolding drama through songs, enactments, and satiric expositions. The chorus in the plays, first of all, play a major role in filling in details of the play's socio-political background, and revealing the inner details or hidden secrets of the protagonists' past. Secondly, the chorus ensures communal or audience participation at emotional, psychological and intellectual levels. Thus, the taunting of Amusa by the women in *Death and the King's Horseman*, the recreation of the Professor-lay reader clash in the Church in *The Road,* its bribery scenes, the downcast mood of the re-enactment of the death of bus drivers like Kokolori, or the torture rituals which vividly recall the reign of terror in several parts of the world but especially in Nigeria during the Civil War are all aimed at eliciting involved responses from the audience. Thirdly, the chorus, by virtue of its composition and other functions highlighted earlier on controls the nature of spectacle, and facilitates the exposition of themes in the plays.

From our analysis thus far, it is clear that Soyinka's dramaturgy entails a myriad of objectives and equally complex technical accessories. To use the words of Adedeji (1987:105), the purpose of Soyinka's theatre is to impart experience "to feel a riddle, to tell a story". This he does through a number of modern theatrical techniques adapted from Western traditions. These include mainly cinematic devices like flashbacks and flashforwards as well as scenic devices. The flashbacks are achieved through a number of means varying from the medium of spectacle as well as mime, music, mask and dance. Together, they all serve the purpose of enhancing both the celebrative as well as the comic mood of the play.

Flashbacks in Soyinka's plays are also realized through verbal re-enactments which involve the characters' verbal recall of events in the past as a means of letting the audience into the background of the characters and events leading to their present condition. Apart from verbal re-enactments and flashbacks through the spectacle of mime, song and dance, Soyinka also uses the conventional flashback through dialogue to achieve a number of objectives. First, it could be a means of establishing historical continuity in stressing the playwright's view of the permanent decadent state of humanity. Thus, if Jones' comments to the effect that "A Dance of the Forests is an attempt to represent the complexities of the human personality and its consequences within this cyclical pattern of history, and that it is a warning against moral complacency and escapism" (1973: 32) is accepted, then the constant recourse to the past through flashbacks becomes essential to the play. Thus, apart from the presence of the dead couple which in itself is a visual and concrete flashback into the past, the court of Mata Kharibu has been consciously evoked by the Forest Head as a reminder of the iniquities which characterize the human past.

Again, flashbacks are also used as a means of externalizing the psychological state of characters. This is amply illustrated in the complex use of the device in The Strong Breed to enact the psychological states of Eman after accepting the responsibility of the Scapegoat in Jaguna's village. In fact, the bulk of the dramatic movements is achieved through the skillfully handled cinematic device of flashbacks. It helps trace the past of Eman's life from when he was a young boy to his present state as carrier.

However, Soyinka's artistic vision does not limit itself to the past and its relationship with the present. To achieve therefore the completion of his deep probings into the human condition, he adopts the use of flash-forward technique. Through this, he is able to show glimpses of the seemingly gloomy future for which he has been criticized by many but which actually is a means of consciously drawing people's attention to the need to break the "recurrent cycle," so as to make possible the realization of his optimistic prognostication. Again, we turn to *A Dance of the Forests* for a succinct example of this in "the Dance of the Half-Child" and the "Dance of the Unwilling Sacrifice" where all representative members of the continuum-the dead, the gods, the spirits and the living-meet in the chthonic realm to decide humanity's future.

Soyinka's communication strategy borrows further from cinematic devices, a means of conveying before the audience a multiplicity of settings which keeps them informed about impending events which may be unknown to the characters themselves. This is the scenic device which enhances the shifting of scenes in quick succession or playing before the audience, actions simultaneously from two opposing settings. The device becomes central in *Kongi's Harvest* where the audience is guided to the various developments leading to the chaos at the end of the play in "Part two". The playwright executes the alternation of scenes through strategic stage notes as we have shown in our analysis in chapter four.

> (The action alternates between two scenes,
> both of which are present and different parts
> of the stage are brought into play in turn, by
> lights. First, Kongi's retreat in the mountains ...)
> (Coloured lights, and the sustained chord of a
> juju band guitar gone typically mad brings on the
> night club scene, and a few dancers on the band itself-,

off stage. Daodu is dancing with Segi)
(*Collected Plays II* : 70-72).

Similar effects are also used in *A Dance of the Forests* where a number of incidents follow one another in quick succession.

However, the theatrical techniques of Soyinka could atimes incorporate a number of these devices within a single breath to achieve maximum communication and enhance his aesthetics. Thus, in the radio play, *Camwood on the Leaves*, Soyinka combines the dream motif with the devices of flashback and flashforward to bring the audience into the proper perspective of Isola's crisis in the play.

Leaving the world of Soyinka's use of ritual as communication strategy and moving on to the aesthetic aspect, it would have become clear by now through our analysis that Soyinka makes use of the whole array of the mechanics of "total theatre". These include songs, music, dance, mime, mask, poetry and cultic aesthetics to evoke the required spectacle and mood in his plays. Thus, we could have a combination of funeral drums and wedding festivities as in *Death and the King's Horseman,* the dirgic songs of *The Road,* the cultic poetry and drums in *Kongi's Harvest* and so on. The resources of language are also fully utilized at all levels; proverbs, aphorisms, symbolism, riddles, and banter are all used as ritual aesthetic strategy. Again, as we have painstakingly established in our analysis in the previous chapters, language in Soyinka's plays represents a central means of character and personality identification.

Thus far, we have traversed the length and breadth of Soyinka's dramatic ensemble focusing on the thematic and formal application of various ritual strategies as dramaturgic imperatives. The picture that is beginning to emerge is of a complex but comprehensive African theatre aesthetics which has remained unrivalled through the decades. We now move on to undertake an analysis of Soyinka's two novels.

PART TWO

THE NOVELS

Chapter

6

THE ANJONU METAPHOR:
TOWARDS A FUNCTIONAL
MAN-COSMOS ORGANIZATION

From this pit of anguish, dug by human hands, from this
cauldron stoked by human hands, from this deafening
clamour, of human hate, the being that emerges is literally
an 'anjonu'. He will return: neither understanding nor
tolerating as before. He will no longer weigh or measure
in mundane terms. Reality for him is forever tinged in the
flames of a terrible passage, his thoughts can no longer
be contained by experiences.

An approach to the analysis of the novelist, Wole Soyinka, as a
socially committed artist can only be successfully undertaken

through a careful study of the "anjonu" metaphor in relation to the two outstanding qualities of creative muse, Ogun, which are creativity and violence. Hence, a brief understanding of both the "anjonu" metaphor and the "Ogunnian" concept will be attempted before going on. This is because what emerges from a fusion of the metaphor and the concept in the life and novels of Soyinka is a dialectical synthesis which explains his social commitment. It also explains his primary purpose of writing for a functional man-cosmos organization through the dual embodiment of the mundane and the metaphysical to project an African world view in his literary products.

The "anjonu" in Yoruba metaphysics is a creature from the 'chthonic realm who with fierce determination commits itself to the regulation of social order. The duality of his function or attitude is visible through his vengeful nature on the one hand and his capabilities for evoking restorative justice on the other. Emphasizing the need to understand the myth of Ogun in any effort to grasp the essence and purpose of Soyinka's novels, Jonathan A. Peters asserts:

> Soyinka's enshrinement of the Yoruba god of war as the central deity of his personal literary credo provides a clue to the fundamental purpose of his undertaking as an artist … (*A Dance of Masks*, 108).

Hence, it can be argued that Ogun's dual facet as god of war and creativity which makes him to be simultaneously representative of violence and creative impulse reflects the writer's ambivalent perception of events in man or a nation's existence. According to the myth, the god's destructive quality, demonstrated in his indiscriminate slaughter of friends and foes during the battle of Ire, characterizes the latent violence in man which, erupting now and then in history, has often resulted in the bloody wars. However, even paradoxically, the major factor responsible for this bloody violence, Ogun's reign as reluctant king of Ire, was itself a reward for his godly daring and manifestation of creative will in bridging the transitional gulf of separation in order to reconnect man with the gods.

Thus, Soyinka believes that it is possible for a regenerative spirit to redeem mankind from savagery through a balancing of his creative achievements in art and society against the precipitation of wanton destruction, violence and carnage as often exemplified in Nigerian society and the world at large. With this in mind, one can readily observe that the works of this writer in early pre and post-independence period are mainly directed towards exposing the factors that could lead to violence in the society while at the same time warning people of the dreadful outcome of such acts. In this connection, *A Dance of the Forest* can be briefly cited as a product of the artist's growing moral awareness early in his career. Soyinka seizes the opportunity of the play, originally written to celebrate Nigeria's independence in 1960, to warn his compatriots of the inevitable outcome, which is war, if society continues to operate only along the lines of ethnic discrimination. Despite this visionary warning, the spate of events in Nigeria in the early sixties only served to confirm the writer's fears. Yet, Soyinka at this early stage of his social commitment refuses to be demoralized or complacent. Rather, he continues to project Nigerian society in all its ugliness and moral sterility in the hope that people would heed his warning. This is the functional purpose of *The Interpreters,* the writer's first novel, published in 1965. The thematic pre-occupations and characterization of this work will now be examined in the light of the already identified objectives of the writer.

A paper on "Modern Black African Society: The Nigeria Scene: A Study of Tyranny and Individual Suppression", which Soyinka delivered at the First World Festival of Negro Arts in Dakar in 1966 highlights the contemporary reality which the writer depicts in *The Interpreters*. The paper provides a rapid summary of the first five years of Nigeria's political independence, 1960 to 1965 thus:

> The trial undergone by the individual had taken on a new
> intensity. It has been more disruptive than under colonial

rule for internal strife has brought with it the shattering
effect of brother betraying brother and the revolt of men
of the same blood. With intellectuals, the case of individual
conscience has taken on tragic dimension... ("Modern
Black African Society", 5).

Drawing on this and other works of Soyinka, Gerald Moore
identifies two prevailing thematic concerns both of which are
very important to an understanding of the artist in the novel. He
is of the opinion that the works of this writer in the mid-1960's
show an underlying fear of the consequences of the violence
which the politicians had roused through the intimidation of their
opponents. Hence the works depict an awareness of the
materialism steadily undermining traditional values and the
indulgence with which corruption and inhumanity are commonly
regarded. Secondly, he believes that all the works of Soyinka
with the exception of *Kongi's Harvest* project, "a profound concern
for the way in which the gods manifest their will both through
human acts and through the contingent moulding of human
personality..." (Moore: *Wole Soyinka*, 45). This second concern
will be examined later on in the chapter under literary techniques
and aesthetics. For now it is important to explore the social vision
of Soyinka in this novel.

The Interpreters focuses on a group of five friends: Egbo, who
works in the foreign office; Sekoni, an engineer and sculptor;
Sagoe, a journalist; Bandele, a university lecturer; and Kola, artist
and university lecturer. Through them, Soyinka depicts Nigerian
society as beleaguered by corruption, hypocrisy, violence and
insensitivity. He also tries to show that individual action, however
meaningful, could positively affect the pattern of life in a morally
bankrupt society.

This is illustrated through Sekoni, one of the interpreters,
who can be described as the star of the black night in which his
society wallows. The level of this character's commitment to the
upliftment of his society could be seen in his determined plan to
technologically transform Nigeria to a modern nation. As a result
of his outburst,

"I realize, minister ch-chairman, that I c-c-cannot con-tinue to be ssigning vouchers and llletters and b-b-bicycle allowances ..." (TI: 26). He is frustrated by the corruption of his superiors in the civil service. His mind is unhinged when he realizes that, because he did not pay the twenty percent kola or bribe, the power station that would have satisfied his fellow country men's demand for energy will never be operated. Before long, this stammerer visionary loses his life in a ghastly motor – accident. Yet, by pouring all his pent-up energy into the art of sculpture, the reactionary violence of the corrupt system turns him into an even more dedicated individual because he is still able to serve as an inspiration to the friends who survive him. This is not the case with the other interpreters.

The interpreters are a group of young intellectuals initially attracted to each other by their youth and idealism and consequently through their individual efforts to carve out moral and ethical values in their society. Confronted however with the cruel reality of their times, all of Sekoni's contemporaries walk away through one of the many doors of escapism - women, sex alcohol, voidancy or act of playing it safe. This can be illustrated further. Egbo is torn between making a dash for the throne at Osa, his home town, and, by implication the smuggling routes which his grandfather controlled on the one hand; and sticking to the bureaucracy of the civil service where he works on the other. Unable to resolve this personal crisis, he seeks escape in wine, women and sex as could be seen in his involvement with Simi and the University girl.

Sagoe, having made a resolution to fight against corruption in high places and determined to stick to the truth in his journalism career starts well initially. He refuses to offer a bribe to secure a job. However, his profession is soon to end in disillusionment and pain when he realizes that "Independent Viewpoint" is much less than being independent. He receives his first shock when Nwabuzor, his editor, prevents pictures of faeces deposited on one of the major roads from being published on the ground that it would "offend the general reader". Later, after doing a painstaking investigation on the official corruption that led to the condemnation of Sekoni's power station, he realizes painfully that this would again not be published because it was a good material for blackmailing the political opponents of the big guns at the "Independent Viewpoint." He gives up defeated and declares, "... I have known all kinds of silence, but it's time to learn some more ..." (TI: 98). Thereafter, he becomes deeply engrossed in his philosophy of voidancy which at least enables him to know that "Shit... next to death is the vernacular atmosphere of our beloved country." This certainly is a submission to the putrefaction which pervades the atmosphere then. The others, Kola and especially Bandele with his mask of "infinite patience," simply have to tag along with the hypocrisy and pretentiousness of their academic community.

But it is not only through the interpreters that the writer portrays this overwhelmingly dark vision of society. For example, the establishment which frustrates the interpreters is characterized by corruption, moral and spiritual decadence. Indeed, those in the upper class of the traditional society like Egbo's grandfather at Osa aid smuggling. The political elite, on the other hand, lack moral values and wallow in corruption. This is well illustrated in Chief Winsala and Sir Derinola, supposedly respected politician and member of the judiciary respectively who instead cheapen their position by engaging in bribe-taking. They both seek bribe from job applicants and even give false morality to their activity by asking Sagoe, a job applicant, to act as a dutiful son to them: "Se wa somo fun wa" (TI: 84).

As for the intellectuals who are supposed to be in the forefront of moral re-awakening in the country, the case is worse. They seem much more interested in worshipping those in positions of power, and this in the hope of being given political appointments. Thus, Ayo Faseyi, one of the best radiologists in the country then, in recounting details of the events at an occasion he attended, is concerned only with the titled. He goes thus: "Do you know a minister was present? Yes, one or two other VIP's ... I saw four corporation chairmen there, and some permanent secretaries" (TI: 203). In the University environment itself, there is moral morbidity. Thus, the students who are only able to produce "uninspired essays" can be seen engaging in immoral sexual activities. Their lecturers who are supposed to be worthy examples to them fare no better because they are hypocritical while the professionals among them lack etiquette. Hence, Dr Lumoye starts the discussion on the pregnant University girl, not out of his desire to condemn the wave of moral corruption among the youths in the country but simply to blackmail the girl for not yielding to his advances. Even Professor Oguazor with his strange British English dialect and his apparent condemnation of "meral terpitude" in the country could not be taken serious. For he himself had a bastard girl well tucked away from society in Islinghton. In fact, the sharp satire inherent in the presentation of these characters will still be fully discussed in the next chapter.

Finally, since the educated middle class – the class of the interpreters which is supposed to organize and act as models for the masses is, to a large extent, impotent and individualistic, the picture cut by the rural and urban masses is far from comforting. Thus, in *The Interpreters* , the masses are projected as either prone to violence – as seen in their attempt to mob Noah; or dubious, as seen in the religious activities of Lazarus and his followers. The rural masses fare no better as they are either gullible, shown in their refusal to allow Sekoni to test the power plant meant for their use, or tribalistic, as shown in the midnight sentimental visit of Dehinwa's relatives apparently to forestall his marriage to a northerner.

However, while it is undeniable that Soyinka's imaginative capturing of events as presented in *The Interpreters* is a true picture of the Nigerian society then and even now, the totally dark social vision he evinces in this novel and his failure to provide a concrete alternative or course for his society appears inadequate. Thus, on the first objection, it can be argued that, despite the overwhelming corruption in the society, there are still some individuals like himself especially the lower class, who still remain unattracted by this bandwagon of moral decadence.

Such people should have been given a place in the novel. Again, even if the group identified above is not in existence then, rather than just presenting the society with "... the choice of a man drowning" (TI: 253), he should have proferred solutions or concrete alternatives to this decadent social order. Hence one cannot but agree, to some extent with the two novelists, Nardine Gordimer and Ngugi wa Thiong'o who have voiced criticisms against *The Interepreters* (Quoted in Ogungbesan, *New African Novel,* 6). On her own part, Gordimer, a white South African novelist, believes that in spite of its perceptive analysis of society, *The Interpreters* "does not suggest a re-ordering of society in political terms as a possible solution..." (Ogungbesan, 6) while Ngugi wa Thiong'o, in stronger terms, criticizes Soyinka for neglecting in the novel "the creative struggle of the masses by not involving his characters in the dialectics of struggle."

In spite of the validity of the claims of these critics, it must be noted that these points are made without a correct perspective or consideration of the situation of things in the immediate post-independence Nigeria where the novel is set. Thus, Soyinka, like other writers in post-colonial African society of this period, believes that a proper stock-taking of the moral state of the society should be presented to the people and politicians with the hope that there would be changes. This is why, in my view, the fact of the spiritual, moral and ethical bankruptcy of the society which the politicians are anxious to cover up is what Soyinka presents in *The Interpreters* and Ayi Kwei Armah in *The Beautiful Ones Are Not Yet Born.* Secondly, on another level, the cautious attitude of this artist towards providing a possible solution in terms of a revolutionary re-ordering of society at this time could be traced perhaps to his understanding of another dimension of the myth of Ogun from which he derives literary inspiration.

This dimension of the Ogunnian concept which has not been highlighted but which is plainly inherent in Soyinka's works is the positive exercise of will which is the supreme act of self-sacrifice. This has the capability of restoring balance to a chaotic and perturbed world which Ogun illustrates by his possession of the will to act positively for mankind by bridging the "abyss of transition" (*Myth, Literature...* 160). A commitment to this concept by Wole Soyinka is an indication of his belief that, though violence might be a necessity for social change, human violence should not be complacently accepted as an irrevocable phenomenon or an end in itself.

Thus, in spite of the isolated activities of this writer as a social activist which sometimes border on violence, a ready illustration of the earlier assertion can be found in his role before and during the Nigerian civil war. Apart from his constant prophetic warning on this impending war, Soyinka strived actively to prevent its occurrence by meeting the leaders of both the federal and Biafran forces to point out to them that the war was only self-destructive and genocidal. Again, during this period he was deeply committed to the concept and ideal of "The third force," as recounted in *The Man Died,* his prison notes. Even this singular act of self-sacrifice for the redemption of his society is one of the major factors that led to his incarceration.

However, historical experience, knowledge of the system as a vicious cycle of violent events, and the writer's moral and personal commitment to the society had already started influencing a re-direction of his social vision by the end of the sixties. This changing vision is reflected in his speech at a gathering of African writers in 1967, thus:

> The time has come when the African writer must have the courage to determine what alone can be salvaged from the recurrent cycle of human stupidity... (*African Concord,* December, 1986, 12).

To hasten the emergence of the revolutionary Ogunnian personality in him, he was arrested by the Nigerian military and held in solitary confinement for more than two years for allegedly constituting a risk to national security. Thus, Soyinka's growing bitterness with the turn of events in the country became aggravated by his imprisonment and this accentuated his resolution and dedication to militancy and non-compromise. In fact, *The Man Died,* published in 1972 after his release, is at once a direct condemnation of the chief actors in the genocidal war and an avowed determination to "… effecting the revolutionary changes to which 1 have become more than ever dedicated…" The text is also a bold re-statement of his present revolutionary state of mind: he declares "I realize also that I moved long ago beyond compromise" (TMD: 9).

Fully drenched by the rain of events, Soyinka now presents a sense of urgency and intensity reflected in his artisitic creations as a weapon aimed at political objectives that could be instrumental in influencing or effecting revolutionary changes. In fact, the level of his social and political commitment at this period can be explained only by the "anjonu" personality evoked in him in prison. The "anjonu" metaphor, as discussed earlier on, has serious implications for this artist who promised to return from his incarceration "neither understanding nor tolerating as before…" This is the mood in which *Season of Anomy ,* the second text to be considered here, was written. Sight must not be lost of the fact that events during the Nigerian civil war as recreated in *The Man Died* informed the writing of *Season of Anomy.* A recourse to the text of the work will help in substantiating the claims outlined above.

Season of Anomy, published in 1973 is Soyinka's second, and last, novel so far and it is often referred to as a sequel to the first, *The Interpreters* published in 1965. In introducing *Season of Anomy*, the thoughts of Bayo Ogunjimi as expressed in his article "Journey, Artifice and Orature: Idioms in Three Revolutionary African Novels" become useful. As Ogunjimi contends, the fear of absolute dictatorship which Soyinka expresses in *Kongi's Harvest* published in 1967 has not been totally fulfilled. However, negation and betrayal of the popular will of the people exemplified in the behaviour of the neo-colonial politicians and the emerging propertied class is already evident in an age of "anomy". However, unlike in *The Interpreters*, the artist in *Season of Anomy* proposes a concrete alternative aimed at establishing a near-perfect social order in society. Thus, one can safely posit that in *Season of Anomy* lies the answer to the various questions he implied in the first novel. The questions border on whether moral sterility and social corruption should continue, or what the possible outcomes of the entrenchment of these social vices in the body politic of the nation can be.

Taking all the above into consideration, Soyinka's thematic pre-occupation in his second novel is the portrayal of warfare, disorder and ruin as inevitable consequences of social corruption, injustice, tribalism and class conspiracy as depicted in the novel and in *The Interpreters*. Furthermore, a careful study reveals that the work is not simply pre-occupied with the depiction of chaos and societal disorder but also with a prognostic anticipation of the kind of society which could emerge from social conflicts which constitutes its subject. The overall thematic concern of the novel is summed up by Ofeyi, one of its central characters who believes that "... the sowing of any idea these days can no longer take place without accepting the need to protect the young seedling, even by violent means ..." (SOA: 23). While this may not mean that he accepts the use of violence like Sembene Ousmane and Ngugi wa Thiong'o, both being writers of Marxist ideological persuasion, Soyinka, in line with his new social vision, appears to be conceding the fact that violence may now and again become an inevitable weapon of rectification of societal imbalance and the rooting out of exploitation.

Consequently, in the work, there is a kind of dialectical relationship between the evolution as well as growth of the progressive idea of Ofeyi, Demakin and the men of Aiyero on the one hand, and the growth of oppressors' hostility and repression as perpetuated by the superstructure of the Cartel, its military cohorts and corrupt traditional rulers on the other. In fact, because of its dialectical nature, some critics have proposed a socialist interpretation of the work. An example of such a critic is Emmanuel Ngara who believes that though critics often emphasize Soyinka's non-alignment to any specific ideological thought, *Season of Anomy* comes very close to expressing commitment to socialist tenets. Quoting Ernst Fischer who has said:

> Socialist art and literature as a whole imply the artist's or
> writer's fundamental agreement with the aims of the
> working class and emerging socialist world (Ngara,
> *Stylistic Criticism*, 99).

Ngara posits that socialist interpretation can be given to *Season
of Anomy* even when its author does not consider himself
committed to socialism. The work will be examined in terms of
the more profound evidence of socialist realism later. For now,
Soyinka's artistic vision can be examined in terms of the points
made above.

A careful study of *Season of Anomy* reveals a clear-cut line of
demarcation between capitalist monopoly and suppression on
the one hand, and progressive communalism, on the other. The
Cartel Corporation and the Mining Trust represent the scourge
of capitalist, exploitation-oriented monopoly seeking to maintain
the status quo set up against the masses of the populace.
Consequently, we witness an unholy alliance between "the purse
and the gun". The military regime in power in the country of the
novel's setting (most likely Nigeria) and the high-ups in the
society including traditional rulers and the moneyed few, collude
to form the status-quo against the generality of the people.
Soyinka lashes out at this class in *The Man Died,* describing them
as the "... self-consolidating, regurgitative, lumpen mafiadom of
the military, the old politicians and business enterprise" (TMD:
1.81).

However, four personalities are brought into focus as propping
up the cartel in *Season of Anomy* and they are Chief Batoki, Chief
Biga, Zaki Amuri and the unnamed Commander-in-Chief who
declares that the hope for "national stability" is in "the alliance
of the purse and the gun..." (SOA138). The forces of progress in
the novel on the other hand are present at two levels. First of
all, at the elementary level by the "unscientific" communalist
ideals of Aiyero and on a higher level by Ofeyi's idea of a
community of workers who will break "the artificial frontiers" of

tribe and region as well as negate "the exploitative activities of the Cartel". A summation of the entire concept can be found in the following sentence in the novel:

> The goals were clear enough, the dream a new concept of labouring hands across artificial frontiers, the concrete, affective presence of Aiyero throughout the land, undermining the Cartel's superstructure of robbery, indignites and murder, ending the new phase of slavery... (SOA: 27).

The fact that the men of Aiyero live by an idea makes Ofeyi feel drawn to them; eventually uniting with them. Thus, a singular progressive vision of opposition to corruption unites Ofeyi, the men of Aiyero and eventually Demakin, the dentist who believes in the systematic elimination of the principal members of the group of exploiters. As the narration advances, the clash between the two forces becomes inevitable.

Furthermore, a critical analysis of this novel reveals ample evidence of elements of social commitment and the inter-relationships between creativity and violence. Here again, one also finds that Soyinka re-creates the Ogunnian character in his work not merely as an artist's eccentric obsession with a god, but because of its relevance to his social vision. Hence, Ogun which in Yoruba cosmology is a wielder of life, a meeting point of opposition; peace and war, order and disorder, creativity and violence can be said to have re-incarnated in Ofeyi. From a broader perspective therefore, the artist's characterization and social vision in *Season of Anomv* could be regarded, to quote Ogunjimi, as "... a creative synthesis of social contradictions and ideals." Thus, one sees that Ofeyi, Demakin and Taiila represent respectively the resourceful creative artist, the violent warrior and the humane aspects of Ogun. Consequently, while Ofeyi and his colleagues see the necessity of turning a state of inertia into mass momentum via the education of the masses "on a truly national scale...," Demakin's vocation on the other hand involves violence. He declares: "I am trained in the art of killing. I utilize this acquisition on behalf of my society ..." (SOA: 111).

It may be ripe indeed to return to a line of argument opened earlier on the possibilities of discovering more elements of socialist realism in this work through a consideration of Soyinka's view on the use of violence in *Season of Anomy*. In my view, while the writer in his quest for a revolutionary and near-perfect or ideal society, concedes to the necessity of political violence, he still holds on to his belief that violence should not be a policy, but only a final resort against a dictatorial establishment perpetrated through the use of violence. This is what Soyinka projects through Demakin, the dentist who sets out to confront violence with violence, "Whoever first invited the other to death literally has his cake and eats it: for the recipient to pretend non-recognition of the invitation accepts his own demise ..." (SOA: 134). The similarity between Demakin's thought and that of a socialist realist like Michael Bakunin who stresses the need to destroy all institutions of oppression in order to create *a* new social order stops here. This is because, henceforth, in most parts of the work, Soyinka maintains a half-hearted attitude towards violence through his characters.

Apparently, the stance of Soyinka is that there is a need for a synthesis of both practical action via violence with revolutionary ideology and prophetic vision. However, events have always proved this stance to be dangerous. Thus, it happened during the civil war that while Soyinka was searching for a means of preventing violence by meeting those concerned with its perpetration, he became exposed to the corruption of the bourgeoisie and the violence committed on innocent people. He realized only too late that this violence needed to be confronted only with violence. His position can be likened to that of Ofeyi, the poet ideologue in *Seagon of Anomy* , who during his mythical search for Iriyise (abducted by the oppressors) learns a bitter but truthful historical lesson, that the process of re-ordering society economically and politically cannot be achieved through the ideology of non-violence. Thus, while witnessing the murderous assault on a congregation of Sunday worshippers at

Cross-river, Soyinka tells us that Ofeyi, "thought of the Dentist at this moment with his rifle and telescopic lens and longed for his precise solution. If even one or two were picked up from this distance, the rest would abandon the attack and flee ..." (SOA: 181).

Furthermore, our knowledge of Demakin's organization of the Aiyero forest camp in Cross-river and the final rescue of Ofeyi, Iriyise and other prisoners in Tiemoko prison (SOA: 316 - 320) show that Demakin has more in him than mere wilful violence and selective assassination. In other words, he is capable of organizing and mobilizing the people for collective action as well as planning for the future rebirth of society.

Hence, our position on Wole Soyinka's rather cautious or half-hearted attitude towards violence is two-fold. The first is that though *Season of Anomy* is a bold re-statement of Soyinka's belief earlier on articulated in *The Man Died* that to achieve a cleansing of society, revolutionary action, even warfare must be combined with a clearly delineated ideological programme. In this regard, there is a lapse. This is in the sense that much of the revolutionary actions in the novel are centred around individuals like Ofeyi as evident in his confrontation with the Cartel Corporation and then Demakin in the pursuit of his counter aggression against the oppressors. They are not concrete and collective actions of the masses who are massacred in various parts of the country. Secondly, the writer's characterization and artistic vision in the work as seen in his simultaneous presentation of Ofeyi, Demakin and Taiila, all of whom represent contradictory aspects of Ogun – creativity, destructiveness and quiescence, appears to justify the liberal humanism claim by many critics with regards to his artistic vision. There is a need for a portrayal of the more revolutionary and less compromising vision of the Ogunnian personality in tune with our contemporary realities. Perhaps, this is to be expected as part of Wole Soyinka's ever-growing social and political commitment.

In the final analysis however, two main contrasts are noticeable in Soyinka's choice of Aiyero and Ofeyi in *Season of*

Anomy who are set against Osa and Egbo in *The Interpreters,* a pointer to the novelist's positive social vision and commitment. Osa typifies the corruption of the past generation with its location controlling several smuggling routes while Egbo, who is entitled to the throne, is faced with the crisis arising between the corruption of the past as represented by Osa or that of the present as typified by the sewage-ridden ports in Lagos and the foreign office where he works. But there is a rejection of the historical vision in *Season of Anomy* because Aiyero (meaning our world has become stable) represents a microcosm of a society in a state of harmony. Socio-mythical affirmation illustrated in the novel in the burial of the old custodian of the Grain could be found at the core of the socio-cultural relationship between Aiyero and its offspring.

Secondly, two separate pictures of the past are presented to us in both novels. In *The Interpreters,* there is a constant argument between Egbo and Sekoni as regards the dead and their pervading presence despite "Egbo's hatred of such knowledge." However, in *Season of Anomy* we are not left in the dark about the writer's stand on such issues when Ahime undertakes to instruct Ofeyi on Aiyero's law of dialectics thus:

> We do not believe in the shackles of memory. We are here to prosper and we know harmony - It is this we teach our children; they grow up despising the dead knowledge of what is gone, dead and rotted (SOA: 32).

This chapter has striven to prove that Wole Soyinka gives a picture of an artist with the creative vision of a better society which could emerge from the rubbles of occasional violence and savagery. A synthesis of the ambivalent attributes of his creative muse and the historically evoked "anjonu" personality in him, presents the picture of an artist committed to his society in his passionate opposition to tyranny and injustice. The complex aesthetics of Soyinka's literary creation which would be examined in the next chapter bears testimony to this assertion.

Chapter

7

❦

AESTHETICS: A DIALECTICAL PARADIGM

Ossie Onuora Enekwe asserts that Soyinka's novels are "... written in obscure and tired language" and with "wayward diction" (Enekwe, 1975, 45). But Niyi Osundare, another known poet and critic contends that Soyinka is essentially " a poet whose drama, essay, prose or formalistic writings are complicated by the cryptic and intensely condensed language that dominates his poetry" ("Words of Iron", 24). These two critics can be said to represent the legion of critical opinions on this writer's obvious linguistic complexity as evident particularly in his two novels. However, the hallmark of the first group of critics to which Enekwe belongs is that they only seek after an inadequate "how" of

Soyinka's language while the second group; that of Niyi Osundare and others, seek a more objective "how" and "why" of Soyinka's "words of iron" and "'sentences of thunder". The approach of the latter group will be adopted here in the study of this writer's use of language because of the obvious pitfall of critics in the former category.

In trying therefore to understand Soyinka's linguistic complexity in his prose, one cannot but turn to what Biodun Jeyifo has identified as the two chief sources of Soyinka's obscurity. The first is that "the pantheon of gods, deities and supernatural beings and archetypal characters" ("Words of Iron", 26) people his work in recurring fashion. The second is that in his novels, there is "elaborate internal, often hermetic language which yields a seemingly inexhaustible panoply of poetic symbols and conceptions" ("Words of Iron", 27). The resultant advantage of these factors is that this artist achieves a tremendous economy of expressions through his self-invented compounds, "private mythology" and compressed metaphors. Examples of such compounds are "tunesmith", "scapeclan", "cloudburst", "houseboat" (*Season of Anomy,* 86) while Soyinka's private mythology could have led to formations like "sky-bull" "earth-bull" (*Season of Anomy*, 15-18). An example of a compressed metaphor can be found in *The Interpreters* where Soyinka says, "Bandele fitted-himself, wall gecko, into a corner." (16)

However, while Niyi Osundare suggests that this author's linguistic complexity is capable of confusing the reader and frustrating his/her attempts to reach an understanding of the text, this essay believes that Soyinka's linguistic strength and complexity is symbolic and relevant to his thematic pre-occupations. Language in his prose works has been turned into a wall of fodder out of the chaotic state of the society. A discussion of the equally complex structure of both novels under consideration which comes next will be used to substantiate this assertion.

A detailed study of the plot of *The Interpreters* has been made by C.O. Awonuga who identifies three types of chapters in relation to the movement of the plot of the novel. These are (a) chapters that carry forward the story in the fictional present without flashbacks to the past, (for example, chapters 8, 11, 12, 16, 17 and 18), (b) chapters which carry forward the present story but which contain flashbacks to the past (for example, chapters 1, 7, 9 and 15) and (c) chapters whose events are chronologically ambiguous to the temporal core of the story. These are chapters (9, 11, 13 and 14).

In partial agreement with some critics like Eustace Palmer and Lewis Nkosi who, obviously frustrated by Soyinka's complicated structuring of his narration, dismissed the novel as either totally lacking in structure or at best as having a weak structure, one can readily observe that the plot structure is complex and demands a frequent readjustment of one's train of thought in following the story. However, the umbilical cord of sympathetic agreement is severed when one considers the fact that it is hardly conceivable that such a plot structure like the language will not have an artistic intent or purpose. Thus, the relevant question should have been: What is Soyinka's artistic intention in employing this technique?

There are two possible answers to this question; the first can be regarded as a theoretical complement to the second which is more relevant to the central pre-occupation of this study. Hence, one could first of all cite Soyinka's address on "The Writer in a Modern African State" delivered to the African-Scandinavian Conference held in Stockholm in 1967. Speaking on the issue of the African writer's noticeable obssession with the past, Soyinka said:

> Of course, the past exists, the real African consciousness establishes this ... the past exists now, this moment, it is co-existent in present awareness. It clarifies the present and explains the future, but it is not a flash point for escapist indulgence, and it is vitally dependent on the sensibility that recalls it ("The Writer in Modern African Society," 11).

From the above, one can see that to Soyinka, the past and present are mutually dependent, that they in fact constitute a continuum. Hence we can see in the plot of *The Interpreters* a "co-existence" or even mutual complementation of the past and the present. The thrust of my argument, therefore, is that this writer utilizes the structural design of his novel as an aesthetic device of illustrating his view of time and history. The importance of this argument in illustrating Soyinka's social commitment is that it calls for a perceptive synthesis of both the past and the present towards a preparation for the future.

Secondly and more importantly, another possible function of the structure of this novel is that of thematic pre-information; in this sense, the plot, like an oryx helps to illuminate the concept of violence in the society as vividly expressed in the novel. Hence, Olukayode Omole ("A Sociolinguistic Analysis of Wole Soyinka *The Interpreters*," 76) in a sociolinguistic analysis of *The Interpreters* sheds light on the fact that the society depicted in the novel is portrayed as one of disharmony, corruption and general disorientation of values. This, according to Omole, accounts for why "Soyinka abandons the naturalistic traditional narrative form" ("Sociolinguistic Analysis," 79). This form, that is, the traditional narrative type, traces events sequentially, and, therefore, implies an order which, unfortunately, this writer believes to be absent in his society. In bare facts therefore, the plot, just like the language already discussed, reflects the complexity and confusion of the modern Nigerian society. The parallel that can be drawn here is that the difficulty of the audience in understanding the message of the work can be compared to the feeling of psychological dislocation and frustration the characters in the novel experience in their society. Correlates of this line of thought can be found in Joseph Frank's paper titled "Criticism: The Foundations of Literary Judgement" where he says:

> When the relationship between man and the universe is one of disharmony and disequilibrium, we find that non-naturalistic, abstract styles, are always produced.

Pehaps it is Soyinka's feeling of disharmony and repugnance towards his morally bankrupt society resulting from his social commitment which accounts for the biting satire which runs through both *The Interpreters* and *Season of Anomy.* Thus, in the satiric swipe of the first novel, Soyinka exorcises societal folly which has given birth to corruption, hypocrisy and confusion of values in the society. For example, in his presentation of the members of the upper class, mostly the intellectuals of the country who still prefer to clown with colonial values, his satire becomes fully realizable. He describes the residential area of the former colonial masters as including "the suburban settlements of Ikoyi where both the white remnants and the new black Oyinbos lived in colonial vacuity" (TI: 112). Moving on to the characters, he presented them in their numbers, the Professor Oguazors, his wife, the Faseyi's and Dr Lumoyes; all intellectuals who should have helped establish good leadership and healthy development in the country but who, instead, embody the confused values of the intellectuals then. Thus Ayo Faseyi , a pseudo-intellectual is concerned with forcing his wife Monica to meet "simple requirements" of the elitist society such as wearing gloves at parties where "even those in native dresses are wearing gloves." At the Professor's party itself, Monica who is actually more attuned to the realities of the country fares better than his intellectual husband who always worships people in high position. Hence, the writer describing the little misunderstanding between Monica and Mrs Qguazor satirically writes "... a black Mrs Professor was faced with the defiance of a young common house-wife, little more than a girl" and for her husband in his usual conceited self, "Nothing kept him earthed but the desperate wish that the floor might open and swallow him" (TI:147).

With the Professor and his wife things are worse. Apart from speaking "a strange dialect of some British tribe," he encourages alienation of the intellectuals from the masses of the people by calling his wife a darling for showing disgust at the sight of an equally black African woman. Though Sagoe is taken aback and asks, "What on earth does anyone in the country want with plastic fruits" when he discovers that what he has mistaken for real fruits are in fact plastic imitations, yet no one aware of the cultural disorientation of the academia in the country then will be taken off balance by the Professor's imitation of European culture.

Furthermore, the corrupt politicians also come under the full glare of Soyinka's satire. At this time in the country, politics is seen as a mere power sharing venture, thus for the "Independent Viewpoint" a newspaper established with public fund, "Lost elections, missed nominations, thug recruitment, financial backing, Ministerial in-lawfulness, Ministerial poncing, general arse-licking, Ministerial concubinage…" (TI:76) accounts for its administrative board. Hence corruption reigns supreme in this establishment as seen in the activities of Sir Derinola and Chief Winsala. Both are ardent bribe takers; while Winsala, an embodiment of corruption among the old generation is seen engaging in open romance with the secretary to the establishment before going for the board meeting. Having passed on, Sir Derinola who is well known for his corrupt practices during his service on the bench is eulogized. This depicts the level of moral sterility in the country. Sagoe feels revulsed by this deliberate falsification of facts by the orator who mouths the panegyric for Sir Derinola thus: "his life our inspiration, his idealism our hopes, the survival of his spirit in our midst the hope for a future Nigeria, for moral irredentism and national rejuvenescence…" (TI: 173).

In this work, Soyinka also criticizes the dubious religious people like Lazarus, the ignorant villagers like Dehinwa's relatives and of course the impotent interpreters who rightly identified themselves as "apostates." However, in *Season of Anomy,* the acerbic searchlight of social criticism is directed at exposing the corruption and criminal activities of the status quo propping the capitalist oriented Cartel Corporations. This can be substantiated by Soyinka's scenic description of events at the Chairman's party. Here, the reader is introduced to the wasteful world of the bourgeoisie when it is learnt that the sole purpose of the extravagant party is to launch "St George" a new water fountain constructed in the compound of the Cartel Chairman. The various groups that have colluded to exploit the common man through the Cartel; the traditional rulers, the politicians, the military rulers are introduced to the readers as they arrived at the party. The show of full military support for the exploitative Cartel Corporation is depicted through the Commandant who had "come with a bodyguard of nearly forty".

However, even more noticeable is the writer's satiric shots at the bourgeoisie through the lyrical composition of Ofeyi such as the nectar and ambrossia verse and other songs. The Pandora Box display which satirizes the four big men of the Cartel Corporation as the scourge of nature brings a shocking climax for those gathered at the party. Other examples of satire proliferate in both novels. This shows the writer's commitment to the exposure of corruption in the society.

Several critics including J.I. Okonkwo (1978) have continued to suggest that there is a close relationship between *The Interpreters* and *Season of Anomy* in all areas of literary and thematic concerns. Therefore, while *The Interpreters* is said to portray a new set of interpreters taking stock of themselves, their problem and the oppressor, *Season of Anomy* shows the implementation of a strategy to confront the oppressor. Consequently, the dialectical nature of Soyinka's aesthetics in *Season of Anomy* has been substantiated by Emmanuel Ngara who claims that:

> The confrontation between the two forces (the oppressor and the oppressed) described above can be more meaningfully understood by studying Soyinka' s use of a sophisticated form ... the use of subtitles with an implied but hidden meaning (*Stylistic Criticism*, 99-100).

Obviously he is referring to the division of the novel into five parts entitled 'Seminal', 'Buds' 'Tentacles,' 'Harvest' and 'Spores'. Each of these parts are a symbolic representation of the growth and fruition of the vision and strategy of the struggle for liberation of the people from their oppressors. The word "seminal" describing the first part refers to the sowing of seeds. It has two chapters which describe how the seeds of a new idea, a new way of life and a revolution moves through the early stages of development. The word "buds" on the other hand, describes the Cartel's programme of suppression and introduces the Corporation as a social blight. It also describes the growth of Ofeyi's programme of undermining the Cartel thus preparing the ground for the on-coming violence. "Tentacles", the third section, vividly describes the development of the civil conflict. It opens with the news of trouble at the Shage dam in Cross River generally, and gives details of the expanding war. The tentacles of the title are the long sinister violence-prone arms of the Cartel. "Harvest" is a relatively brief section, which describes varied harvest of violence, hate and destruction. Finally, "Spores" depicts the outcome of violence engendered by the first round of the war. Here, there is a recreation of the effects of stress on life in the form of grotesque and socially, emotionally and physically handicapped individuals who occupy Tiemoko, both gaoler and the gaoled. Their deformities are symbolic of those of the society in general. This brings us to the end of the text, as the revolutionaries prepare to retreat to Aiyero, "the walls and boarders shed their last hidden fruit. In the forests, life began to stir" (SOA: 230).

Another important point of relationship between *The Interpreters* and *Season of Anomy* which also helps in revealing the growing social commitment of Soyinka as well as his portrayal of the inter-relationships between violence and creativity is Sagoe's philosophy of voidancy, characterized by shit and vomit which is a scatological technique used by the writer to make an important social statement. His message is that to achieve social, psychological and spiritual cleansing of the society, there is a need for the destruction or purgation of evils so that the birth of the good or renewal of society can be effected. This is the essence of the voidance dialectics as summarized by Sagoe in *The Interpreters*:

Voidancy is not a movement of protest, but it protests! It

is non-revolutionary, but it revolts. Voidancy – shall we
say – is the unknown quantity. Voidancy is the last
uncharted mine of creative energies, in its paradox lies
the kernel of creative liturgy. In release is birth (TI:70).

However, developed in line with Soyinka's revolutionary
intention in *Season of Anomy*, Sagoe's theory of voidancy now
transformed into a functional and purposeful philosophy which
matches the dentist's dialectical concept of extracting the "carious
tooth" quickly before it infects the others.

Obviously, Demakin the dentist is referring to his philosophy
of systematic elimination of the exploiters and oppressors in the
society.

Generally, flashbacks which form a common feature of
Soyinka's prose writings, serve the purpose of filling in details.
For example, the characters and plot of *The Interpreters* "jump
to and fro" without any clear mode of transition. Flashbacks are
then used to illustrate how they arrive in their present situation.

Furthermore, because of the episodic nature of the novel,
events taking place at various settings as well as the characters
involved can only be presented through the use of flashbacks.
Lastly, another identifiable function of flashbacks especially in
Season of Anomy, is that of showing the writer's notion of history
as a recurring process. This can be illustrated through Soyinka's
narration of the slave raiding activities of Cross-River in the past
and its present hostilities against Aiyero.

Of Myth, Allusions, Allegory and Archetypes

As Gerald Moore contends in his book titled *Wole Soyinka*, one
of the issues lying at the centre of *The Interpreters* is "a profound
concern for the way in which the gods manifest their will both
through human acts and through the contingent moulding of
human personality" (*Wole Soyinka*, 35). Consequently, it is
through the central characters that one understands the tension
and harmony of the Yoruba cosmogony/cosmology which
Soyinka deploys in drawing attention to the chaotic state of

contemporary Nigerian society in which the novel is set. This is revealed through the unfolding encounters of the "interpreters" in the society and mainly through Kola's attempt at artistically recreating the Yoruba pantheon of the gods.

In fact, Kola's pantheon is a major aesthetic ploy for depicting and satirizing the lack of direction and chaos in the society then. This chaos is in fact the politics of Kola's pantheon because the once unified pantheon has been split into a thousand fragments following an act of rebellion by Atunda who is the helper of "orisa-nla", the principal deity. The result of the singular act of "apostasy" by Atunda is chaos and tension necessitating a continuous search for harmony in Yoruba cosmology. However, as a result of the persistent failure of the gods to achieve harmony in the cosmos, chaos reigns supreme and this is reflected in the text through the portrayal of the personal crisis of each of the interpreters as well as that of the Nigerian society. For example, each of the four leading characters in the novel can be seen as allegorical or representative figure in the Yoruba pantheon.

Consequently, Egbo with his love for palmwine and adventure, is Ogun the god of violence and creativity; Sagoe, though often childish but always acting the wily trickster is Esu, the god in Sekoni, the whipping boy of corruption and an electrical engineer who has to go through suffering is Sango, god of lightning, and Bandele who often times is the protector of the group of friends as well as their conscience is Obatala or Orisa-nla, the god of creation. As R.K.Priebe asserts in his work, since the friends or the interpreters themselves possess the characteristics of those gods, "they may be seen as priests who have the responsibility of serving the gods that possess them" ("Development of Mythic Consciousness in African Literature," 78).

Bearing this in mind therefore, one is not surprised by Soyinka's portrayal of them as essentially monomaniac characters, who are engaged more with personal or monomaniac characters' individual crises than with the societal one as discussed earlier on in this work. By way of resolution however, only the ultimate sacrifice of Noah through the homosexual advances of

Joe Golder is strong enough to bring the friends together once again and awaken in them the need to reconcile their personal differences so as to be able to deal with the problems of the society. In the case of Nigeria, the setting of the novel, only the bloodshed that attended the civil war can engender renewal. This is the concern of *Season of Anomy* already discussed to a large extent in the last chapter.

The claim that Wole Soyinka's employment of aesthetic elements in *Season of Anomy* is dialectical and illustrative of social commitment can be further confirmed using Mazisi Kunene's contention to the effect that myth "can organize the historical contents in terms of perspectives," and "recreates an attractive vision defining in familiar cosmic terms the future possibilities of society" ("Relevence of African Cosmological System to African Literature ," 190-191). Thus, through Soyinka's use of myth, there is a re-creation of the pathfinder's role of Ogun through the testy trials of the "chthonic realms" in Ofeyi's search for Iriyise. Soyinka himself has defined the "chthonic realm" as "the seething cauldron of the dark world will and psyche, the traditional yet inchoate matrix of death and becoming." (*Myth, Literature*, 142) Furthermore, there is an expansion of the writer's myths and allusions in consonance with his revolutionary pre-occupation in the novel through his recreation of the Greek mythology involving Orpheus and his lover Eurydice in Ofeyi's mythical search for Iriyise. The emerging social vision and aesthetic articulation is further confirmed by Ogunjimi when he stresses that Soyinka "wields mythical and political allegories and makes moral thesis out of them" ("Journey, Artifice and Orature," 7).

The central stylistic device for discussing the use of myth in this work is the journey artifice which makes possible the creative link between the Ogunnian character Ofeyi and the Orpheus – Eurydice myths. Thus, Soyinka makes use of allegory as a means of sensitizing man to events in his environment as could be seen in the concept of the archetypal figure represented in Ofeyi who undergoes a quest in his search for Iriyise and wages a battle against the Cartel. But in the process, he acquires new knowledge which forces him to align with others like Demakin in order to rescue humanity from total degeneration and disintegration though not without going through and witnessing distressful human condition. In fact, this position is analogical to Soyinka's personal experience during the war as earlier discussed. For Ofeyi and Zaccheus therefore, the journey artifice becomes a set of rites of passage which will ensure the opening of new insights to them. Thus, Ofeyi explains to Demakin who considers the journey suicidal:

> ... every man feels the need to seize for himself the enormity of what is happening at the time in which it is happening. Perhaps deep down I realise that the search would immerse me in the meaning of the event, lead me to a new understanding of history (SOA: 218).

The journey itself is not a pleasure drive through a beautiful town but the journey through Cross-river area presents an agonizing picture of the conspiracy of traditional rulers, the tribal political leaders and the genocide prone army against the generality of the people who became wanton victims of reactionary violence. The convulsive feeling of nightmare is transferred from the protagonists to the reader as savage terror grips the land in "Harvest." For example, from pages 196-201 of the text, we witness the assault on Sunday worshippers at Kuntua. On page 207, we learn that Captain Magari was shot while "trying to stop some of the army boys from shooting civilians." On page 229 we encounter the "horribly gashed and mutilated poor man "in person of the senior nurse murdered in cold blood while from pages 230 - 234, we are taken on a heart-numbing round of the mortuary where there is "no more room" because "it filled up in no time at all." On page 154, the protagonists and the readers witness a violent ritual killing while the situation at Shage and Temoko where both the gaoled and the gaoler are psychologically handicapped cannot be easily wiped off memory.

Hence, an exposure to this kind of reactionary violence by Soyinka forces on him the need to organize a return aggression against the oppressors. This could be seen in *Sea so n of Anomy* through the progressive violence proposed by Demakin as a means of rescuing human society which is the kind of violence associated with Ogun. In fact, in terms of archetype, Demakin in this role can be seen as embodying the activist, warlord and creative pathfinder aspects of Ogun who uses his iron ore to bridge the "abyss of transition." This could be seen in the fact that Demakin does not stop at violence alone, he organizes and directs the movement for resistance against reactionary violence and declares after engineering the emancipation of the inmates of Temoko, "I have already turned my mind to the strategy for the future" (SOA: 219).

Soyinka's use of myths and allusions does not stop with the classical Orpheus-Eurydice myth. Contemporary historical facts and events as well as relevant references to world literature and biblical stories also inform the work. For example, many of the events that are recreated in *Season of Anomy* are drawn from occurrence recorded in *The Man Died*, the writer's prison notes. Consequently, we are not surprised when Dr. Chalil relates the story of the Asian attendant brought to a Cross-river hospital to practise surgery – "butchery" by Zaki. Here, the writer is referring to his earlier expose on the late Sardauna of Sokoto who was mostly responsible for the importation of mediocre talents into the country then. Furthermore, there are references to Anubi's resurgence in Ofeyi's dream on pages 15-160. Anubi itself is taken from ancient Egyptian mythology and Tarzan "the ultimate primate of colonial fantasies" on page 168 of the text.

Biblical references also proliferate in the novel. For example on page 221 through Ofeyi's mind "which jumped to Herod's desperation for infanticide" on the entrance to the morgue one is forced to draw a parallel to the Cartel's massacre of innocent workers. Thus, Soyinka once again employs dialectical aesthetics to demonstrate his social commitment.

In sum, Soyinka's complex aesthetic elements in *The Interpreters* and *Season of Anomy* are examined in this chapter as dialectical paradigms used to communicate his equally complex social vision and project the ambivalent attributes of his creative muse, Ogun.

Chapter

8

SOCIAL AND IDEOLOGICAL
COMMITMENTS: THE DIVIDING
LINES IN THE NOVELS OF
WOLE SOYINKA

Ezekiel Mphahlele in his paper titled "Writers and Commitment"
asserts that:

> Every writer is committed to something beyond his art, to
> a statement of value not purely aesthetic, to a 'criticism
> of life' (Mphahlele, "Writers and Commitment", 3-7).

Though the study of Wole Soyinka as a socially committed artist
in this book is not premised on this rather simple observation of

Mphahlele, the excerpt is meant to establish that there are various facets of commitments. Thus, this chapter attempts to draw the dividing lines between social commitment and ideological commitment as reflected in Soyinka's writings. This is borne out of the discovery that several critical works encountered in the course of this research work approach Soyinka from an ideological perspective from which the writer himself has not approached his writing. The result is that the man's works are either condemned or that the writer is attacked for failing to show specific socio-political ideological commitment in his work. Again, this chapter seeks to prove that the writer has greater pre-occupations which transcend ideological limitation.

Thus, social commitment as examined in this work can be described as a natural process stemming from a prior dedication to specific social and political issues by a writer or individual. At the beginning of our discussion of Soyinka's novels, we established that Soyinka is a socially committed artist whose commitment stems from morality rather than a subscription to any ideology, whether literary or political. Hence, in an interview with John Agetua, a Benin based publisher in 1975, Soyinka stresses his belief in "an egalitarian society uncompromisingly characterized by equal justice, economic welfare and the right of each individual to achieve maximum fulfillment" (*African Concord*, No 121, p. 11). This belief has always been the guiding principle of his literary and social life. However, the refusal to root this vision of society in a specific ideology has often pitched him against the legion of ideologically committed artists and critics of Marxist orientation like Niyi Osundare and especially Ngugi wa Thiong'o who labelled him a liberal humanist (see *Writers in Politics*, 65). Our intention here is not to engage in abstract definitions of what ideological commitment or Marxism is, but to conduct a meaningful examination of the social vision of a writer/critic like Ngugi wa Thiong'o as a fertile expression of committed artistry.

This expression could be found in *Writers in Politics* where Ngugi approaches an understanding of the historical realities of

Africa as well as the role of the committed writer from a Marxian dialectical perspective. Says he in the book on the question of how the writer projects the "historical drama" his community is undergoing:

> The fundamental opposition in Africa today is between imperialism and capitalism, on the one hand, and national liberation and socialism, on the other: between a small class of native "haves" which is tied to international monopoly capital and the masses of the people (78).

Ngugi insists that the role of the writer is felt within the scope of how he explains this world situation and how he depicts the economic and political struggle of the masses against the established status quo of the bourgeoisie and the political cum cultural system protecting it. His call then is that the African writer must show commitment which goes beyond abstract beliefs in justice and peace, but portrays the struggle of the African people against the various forces of oppression and the need to adopt socialism as an alternative social system. Then in what looks like a direct indictment of writers of indistinct ideological stance like Soyinka, he declares that "faced with these contradictions, the African writer can often retreat into individualism, mysticism and formalism" (*Writers in Politics*, 79).

The fundamental opposition between the two identified facets of commitment can however be located within the perspective of the distinction between critical realism and socialist realism which dictates differences on the level of *attitude* and *method* of writers. Arnold Kettle has made a distinction between the two thus:

> Critical Realism ... means literature written in the area of class society from a point of view which, while not fully socialist, is nevertheless sufficiently critical of society to reveal important truths about that society and to contribute to the freeing of the human consciousness from the limitations which class society has imposed upon it ... Socialist Realism ... means literature written from the

point of view of the class-conscious working class, whose socialist consciousness illuminates their whole view of the world and of the potentialities of mankind ("Dickens and the Popular Tradition", 214).

The basic difference therefore between the socially committed and the ideologically committed writer could be found in the difference Olu Obafemi draws in "Commitment, Anguish and the Search for Catharsis: Nigerian Writers and the Civil War," an MA dissertation he submitted to the University of Sheffield in 1978, between both in terms of attitude and method. On the level of attitudes, all writers, whether critical or socialist realists, are sufficiently aware of the objective realities of societies. They show repugnance to the obscene bourgeois structure which succeeded colonialism, the corruption and moral sterility that pervades the atmosphere in their various societies, and ethnic politics which has led to civil strife in some countries like Nigeria. In contrast however, and at the level of methods, the critical realists approach their literary and social life from the individualist perspective. In other words, such writers produce literary works in which focus is placed on the efforts put forward by individuals to achieve revolutionary feats for the society. Even in their social live, such writers often oppose the status quo passionately through different activities. Yet these are not enough to uproot the system they attack. At times such writers endanger their own lives. For example, Soyinka's active involvement in political activism during the Nigerian crisis led to his incarceration by the military government then. But the socialist realists on the other hand, seek a radically changed society through creation of works showing the potentialities of the collective struggle of the oppressed all over the world in obtaining a change. This is the kind of challenge that Ngugi places before African writers.

However, it is our view in this work that understanding Soyinka's social and literary life can only be achieved through the appreciation of the value he attaches to the individual. Soyinka sees the writer as an individual who may realize his abilities to inspire and thereby move others, inviting them to imbibe his view point and standards as he has shown them through his works. Hence, after reading the text, the individual has the choice of acting on his standards or rejecting them. This writer himself tries to inspire his audience by providing insights into the human condition, illuminating issues of contemporary social relevance as he has done in *The Interpreters* and *Season of Anomy*. In short, Soyinka's centre of focus is the individual as he asserts in an interview:

> It is the individual working as part of a social milieu and this may be a fluctuating milieu ... who raises the consciousness of the community of which he is part ... I believe implicitly that any work of art which opens out the horizon of the human mind, the human intellect, is by its very nature a force for change, a medium for change (*In Person*, 86).

But we have shown in a chapter of this work through an examination of *The Interpreters* that individualist attempts to salvage society could be fraught with dangers. In fact, Soyinka's fate in the civil crisis has shown the risks of this individualist vision. Hence, on being exposed to the evils being perpetrated by the status quo in Nigeria in *The Man Died*, he declares: "I did and still wish that the revolt in the West had achieved victory as a people's uprising ..." (161). However, such late wishes cannot achieve result, except that of a better social vision in *Season of Anomy*.

In chapter six of the work, through an analysis of the thematic preoccupations of both novels under consideration, we have shown the relationship between them as indicative of the writer's growing social commitment. In fact, considering the differences between *The Interpreters* and *Season of Anomy* which, apart from depicting the situation of the country then also puts forward concrete proposals for revolutions, we have considered both in terms of ideological progression. Thus, *The Interpreters* can be regarded as a work of critical realism while *Season of Anomy*, to a large extent, is a work whose creation has been informed by socialist realism. The difference between the two has been explained earlier on.

However, further analysis of even *Season of Anomy* reveals the short comings of trying to force the critical concerns of Marxist criticism on works whose production transcends ideological concerns. Thus, a consideration of Soyinka's views on, and the use of, violence reveals a line of demarcation between this writer's intentions and the notion of violence in socialist literature. But it is in chapter seven where this work establishes that Soyinka's use of a complex aesthetic matrix in his prose is a reflection of the multiple dimensions of such works as well as an indication of complex but unique social vision of this writer.

Hence, believing the author's work must be understood in its own terms, this work puts forward a number of arguments in chapters six and seven some of which can be summarized here. The first of them is that Soyinka is not only concerned with the criticism of modern society; rather, his literary critical base could be found in the much more valuable evaluation of both traditional and modern practices. This stems from the writer's belief that a concern with either.the past or present alone is inadequate. What is needed for preparing the future is a synthesis of both the past and the present to achieve the ideal society. Thus, in his commitment to the necessity for positive change in the society, the writer presents us with a scathing condemnation of both the past and the present state of the country's life in *The Interpreters* and with an idealized model in *Season of Anomy*.

Secondly, Soyinka's metaphysical insight into the necessary and inevitable interrelationship between violence and creativity as examined in chapters six and seven of the study reveals the more profound social vision of this artist while at the same time providing us with the informing factors of his attitude toward violence. Thus, an understanding of the essential attributes of Ogun, the artist's creative muse which are creativity and violence reveals that violence, paradoxically, is essentially inherent in humanity. However, Soyinka's stand is that the factors which can precipitate the eruption of violence both in man and in the society can be consciously curtailed and controlled by the committed individual. This is the intention of the writer in *The Interpreters* where he undertakes a visionary exploration of those factors which at that time were speeding Nigeria to the path of civil war such as moral turpitude, corruption, insensitivity and tribalism.

Even on the question of the necessity to use violence to challenge the status-quo in society which makes a functional man-cosmos organization impossible such as exploitation and corruption, Soyinka, as shown in the work, calls for a positive exercise of will. Thus, his belief is that though violence can sometimes become a necessity for achieving revolutionary change in society, indiscriminate violence must not be accepted as a policy. This explains that though Ogun represents for the artist the negation of complacence and cowardice, his views about violence is more thoughtful as depicted in *Season of Anomy*. Soyinka believes that while being actively destructive for revolutionary purposes, thoughts must also be given to how to be actively creative.

Perhaps this accounts for his constant opposition to the apparent enthusiasm of some so called ideologically committed artists for revolution. Soyinka declares in a published interview:

> I would rather not be bracketed with those pseudo-Stalinists and Marxists who are totally unproductive and merely protect themselves behind a whole barrage of terminologies which bear no relation to the immediate needs of society (*African Concord*, 11).

His opposition to literary and religious ideology had earlier on been stated in *Myth, literature and the African World* where he says, "a social vision, yes, but not a literary ideology" (61) when asked about the necessity for a literary ideology. This is because, according to him, "the formulation of a literary ideology tends to congeal sooner or later into instant capsules which, administered also to the writer, may end up asphyxiating the creative process ..." (61).

Since the literary writing which fosters such ideologies cannot objectively evaluate its systems of belief. The resultant effect is that when such reigning ideology vigorously projected without having first being consciously scrutinized fails to fulfill or retain its false comprehensive adequacy, it is discarded (62).

Thus, it can be argued that this writer's social vision is directed in his works towards inspiring a well guided revolution which will lead to the emergence of a society more specifically African as well as modern. He believes that the best of traditions can be wedded to communalism in the process of reordering a state. This view forms the thematic and aesthetic basis of both *The Interpreters* and *Season of Anomy*.

Chapter

9

❦

CONCLUSION

RITUAL, VIOLENCE AND SOCIAL TRANSFORMATIONS: A LION OR A JEWEL?

In the first part of this book, we discussed Soyinka's perspective of ritual and social transformation as articulated in a selection of his dramatic works. Undoubtedly, African drama has its roots in the communal rituals aimed at propitiating forces inimical to man's existence on this terrestrial plane. However, the drama, like African literature generally, registered its presence in modern world literature with the advent of contemporary playwrights of Africa who create largely in European languages.

Each of these pioneer playwrights, usually university trained, instantly become a child of two worlds: of the traditional African heritage, on the one hand, and the Western education which predisposes him to existing Western theatrical modes, codes and concepts on the other. As self appointed cultural ambassadors responding to the prevailing racial climate of the period, these dramatists were conscious of a need to create a distinct, modern African theatre. Mahood (1966:27) sums up the feeling of these African dramatists:

> There is a growing awareness among African playwrights that they also need to achieve some synthesis of the old and the new, the indigenous and the foreign, if they are ever to produce a distinctively African drama for the modern theatre world. But a synthesis is something less easy to achieve than a mere mixture.

Perhaps we ought to pause straight away to recognize the contribution of the residual artists. The only probable connection of these residual artists with Western theatrical forms was the gradual transfer of their plays from the village square and open places into halls and proscenium stages specially designed for such activity. The residual repertory, essentially consists of indigenous oral performances, vernacular performances and the folk operatic theatre. The resource base for their creations are history, legends, myths, the mystic realm and a few plays centred on contemporary issues. Foremost among these dramatists were Duro Ladipo, Hubert Ogunde, Kola Ogunmola, all practitioners of the traditional dramatic form to use the classification of Ogunbiyi (1981:10). However, Mahood's observation primarily concerns playwrights in the literary tradition. This group of playwrights finds inescapable the trap of adapting Western models to suit African settings. One such playwright provides a ready example. James Ene Henshaw, set on creating African plays, merely ended up producing plays modelled after British comedies while treating African issues.

Contemporary playwrights are the heir apparent of these dual directions in African drama both of which are inadequate on their own to fulfill the aspirations of the university trained dramatists who have been exposed to the modern literary world where drama does not end as stage activity but is a subject of scholarship with supporting theories of criticism. The most obvious solution for these writers is to develop as individuals their own approaches to the interpretation of the African traditional heritage and the European influence to create versions of what collectively emerge as African drama.

In most cases, the above entails a conscious blend of international classical forms with the indigenous arts, myths and rituals. A good case in point is J.P Clark's trilogy *Song of a Goat*, *The Raft* and *The Masquerades*. Although they all take their thematic and dramaturgic materials from his Ijaw traditional environment, they still structurally follow the classical recommendations on tragedy. However, skillful handling of traditional resources especially ritual as noted by Ashaolu (177-199) cannot be denied. Others like Ola Rotimi, Zulu Sofola, Wale Ogunyemi, Ama Ata Aidoo have also exploited the potentials of ritual drama to make dramatic statements through experimentations mainly in the tragic mode. Mahood (1966:27) again assesses Nigerian dramatists' achievements in this area:

> The difference between drama., which is African only in its setting and which has been liberated from traditional European literary forms through the playwright's study of modern theatrical experiments can be illustrated by Nigerian works.

However, the most accomplished among them is the playwright under study. Searching in the early sixties for a theoretical foundation for his blossoming creative outputs, Soyinka burrowed into the abyss of Yoruba mythology armed with skills acquired through exposure to existing dramatic theories:

> I have long been pre-occupied with the process of

apprehending my own world in its full complexity (*Myth, Literature*: ix).

The dramatist emerged with a literary philosophy which synthesized his choice of earlier Western dramatic theories with the African metaphysical sensibility to create a sustained paradigm both for his works and the entirety of modern African theatre. The theory is predictably complex and is woven around the exploits of Ogun, the bifaced avatar of destruction and creativity. However, its main dramaturgic form is ritual:

> Ritual is a metaphor for the perennial, and the perennial is not located in any one such and such events. Birth is a perennial event so is death. So are courage, cowardice, fear, motion, rain, drought, storm … Ritual is the irreducible formal agent for event- disparate and time-separated actions of the human being in human society... (Soyinka "Who is Afraid of Elesin Oba?": 110).

We have dwelt sufficiently on the details of this theory and its manifestations in relating rituals to tragedy and social consciousness. What remains at this point is a critique of its worth based primarily on the strength of our textual analysis and other seemingly endless critical responses to it. It is generally agreed that Soyinka's theory of ritual drama is sound and viable. According to Ogunba (1975:1), "Soyinka is a skillful dramatic poet and theatre technician and the sheer artistry of his plays has fascinated many people who know rather little of his subject matter." Osofisan (1978:156) also believes that Soyinka's creations thus far possess two major connecting threads: "a seriousness and consistency of theme, and the gradually ripening use of theatre mechanics…" Several other critics notable among whom are Eldred Jones and James Gibbs have also praised Soyinka's drama. A summation of the achievements of the dramatic theory and plays of Soyinka has been given by Sensalo (1970:17):

> He manages to discuss universal themes of conflict between the community and the individual, conflicts

between old and new, life and death, myth and reality, custom and progress, apartheid, etc. ... all against a truly African background. His plays are Africanness mingled with universality. As Martin Esslin observes, Soyinka has managed to write about Africans; in an African social context, African peasants who in reality speak their own African languages in the medium of an alien stage and an alien language.

However, criticisms of Soyinka's artistic vision and dramaturgy also abound. These are isolatable as emanating from three perspectives. First is the questioning of the adequacy of the metaphysical milieu on which the artist's theoretical constructs has been built. Secondly, there is the emerging artistic vision of Soyinka and lastly there is the issue of the accessibility of the entire gamut of his ritual dramaturgy. The first need not waste our time. The core argument has been aptly described by Jeyifo (1988:177) as the "academicist critique of Soyinka's philosophy of culture". Foremost among these critics are Anthony Appiah, as exemplified in his "Soyinka and the Philosophy of Culture", and Isidore Okpewho, a renowned oral literature scholar. The essence of their query of Soyinka's theoretical construct, to quote Jeyifo again, "pertains to what is perceived as the inadequacy of basing an account of the traditional African worldview primarily on Yoruba mythology and world view" (177).

The case of these scholars, though noteworthy, can be summarily dismissed when the unassailable fact is considered that the necessity is a theory which, apart from comprehensively apprehending the black man's milieu, also fosters the prospect of social and revolutionary consciousness in the face of several centuries of Eurocentric debasement. In any case, a proper apprehension void of deceptive generalization could only have been done from the cultural milieu Soyinka is most familiar with; the Yoruba, just as many other writers have done using their own cultures.

If this criticism can perhaps be readily set aside, others cannot. A powerful critique stems mainly from critics of Marxist ideological persuasion and a few non-ideologically committed ones. They assert that the sustained vision emerging from Soyinka's works, no matter the theme being treated is essentially pessimistic, a direct result of his interpretation of history as a "recurrent cycle of human stupidities". In other words a charge of stasis hangs on Soyinka's artistic vision, a position maintained by the likes of Andrew Gurr (1988:139-145) and Osofisan (1974:53):

> The tragic mood colours all of Soyinka's works, constantly creeping in behind the laughter. In his poetry, novels and especially in the plays, the images are all of death, decay and rust, of horror and dismay, of transient "grey" essences, of sacrifice and betrayal. There is rarely tenderness but recurrent violence, rarely love but much lust and ecstasy, rarely peace but always the menace of iron, the treachery and turbulence of the road ...

This is such that even for a play in which Soyinka deliberately subverts a classical tragedy The Bacchae of Euripides for revolutionary intent via the medium of ritual, Adebayo Williams (1981:42) still has no difficulty locating a problem. To him, "it is in its obstinate stasis, its striving to weld contemporary actuality to fit into the chassis of mythology that Soyinka's system suffer as a potent weapon of social redemption."

Leaving for a moment the endless defence put forward against the charge by Soyinka and his acolytes, a critical review of human existence in the universe and especially Africa, will show that the reality-recurrent wars, coups, natural hazards and violence of the modern world can hardly generate any other feelings than the pessimistic. True, the artist as the voice of vision in his time ought to point to brighter horizons and hopeful beginnings; this has never been absent in Soyinka's plays and we have taken pains to establish this point in our analysis. Soyinka definitely preaches change but not through the simplistic path of imposing fore-determined idealistic conclusions on situations. For him the starting point is the "piercing of the encrustations of the soul deadening habits to bare the mirror of original nakedness." To break the Karma of cyclic tragedy a regenerative and communal process must be set in motion, but to deny its causes would be to deny the obvious. As Soyinka himself has remarked:

> All humanity seeks power and to have power you must have victims. Victims are power made manifest. It's human nature; but I am not a pessimist. The more one recognizes these truths of imperfection the greater is my impulse to refuse to accept them. It's a contradiction if you like. It's illogical. But then human nature isn't governed by logic (*The Guardian*, London, 1972).

The other aspect of Soyinka's artistic vision is the constant probing, a metaphysical concern with transition, the intricate issues of life and its complementary parity - Death. Again the issues are basic to our existence except we consciously brush them aside in search of the bright light:

> Nobody, I hope, will tell us that the fear of death or, at the very least, the resentment the sense of unpleasantness about death is simply due to the environment. My suspicion is that this need to communally contain Death will always be there. No matter the historico-materialist incantation of the Marxist ("Who's Afraid of Elesin Oba": 127).

Perhaps, we should now turn to the criticism of Soyinka's ritual dramaturgy as pertains to its mechanics and accessibility. Hepburn (1988:593), making a comparison of three ritual plays by Soyinka, makes the following incisive observations:

> Of these three ritual plays, though, *The Strong Breed* may be the most inaccessible to Western audiences because ritual is the whole concern in this play. In *The Road* are comedy, corruption, and other issues which Soyinka subordinates to the main action and theme, but which engage his audience more. Also, Samson's linguistic power, his colourful character so dominates the play that the less understood egungun elements are not so highly visible in *The Road* ... In *A Dance of the Forest* too, language

and characters like Rola lend interest and levity to the drama and to the otherwise difficult to understand ritual symbolism of the play; but in *The Strong Breed*, where the ritual is all-important, audience interest may not be so high.

This comment can to a large extent be said to be true for even African audiences which for now is made up of the élite – teachers, undergraduates and scholars of the ivory towers among whom sparse productions of some of these plays take place. The production of *The Road* directed by Femi Osofisan which ran for several nights in September and November 1990 at the Arts Theatre Ibadan, grants us some insights into the audience reception of a ritual drama. Night after night, a significant number of the audience spoken to confessed their difficulty in grasping the metaphysical postulations of Professor but really enjoyed the satiric enactments of Samson and Salubi. Thus, the situation would have been worse in a play like *The Strong Breed* where no such enactments exist.

However, this could be said only of *The Strong Breed* which as we noted earlier leans heavily on Western classical notions of tragedy. African tragedy as Soyinka was to realize later does not banish humour and laughter from the stage. Hence, in all other plays, he has infused elements of humour, satire and comedy as part of the ritual communication and aesthetic strategy aimed at inducing intellectual participation just as the metaphysical elicits emotional and empathic blurring of the stage-audience dichotomy. Again, it is plausible to agree with Cook (1987:89-103) who argues on the basis of practical experience obtained in East Africa that the problem with Soyinka's plays is not totally its metaphysical or ritual contents, but the absence of interested producers who could take the plays before rural and popular audiences than elitist audiences "trying to piece together its symbolism and interpret its message".

Directly linked with the above problem is the question of language in the plays of Soyinka which, as we said earlier, operates at several levels. The first is the language of the tragedies which draws from subliminal resources. Words here are taken back to their roots where music and poetry merge to evoke images, allusions and numinous essences to contain the tragic passage. At a second level is the ordinary use of language which deeply reflects the status of the speaker. Examples here range from the dignified language of Forest Head, to the silence of Murano, the abstractions of Professor and Kongi's cult, to the carefree language of Samson and the layabouts. Adrian Roscoe (1971:244) has observed Soyinka's recognition of the impact and exploration of language to create intellectually satisfying play-texts and theatre:

> Thus we can understand Soyinka's fundamental interest in language. Language as a key to man's inner being; language as a mirror of social standing; language as an instrument of deceit and oppression; language as a vehicle for man's deepest utterances; language as a source of comedy; language as an instrument of satire ... Soyinka is keenly aware of all these facets and explores them energetically in his plays.

Yet, Soyinka has often taken the knock on the head from critics who are always anxious to generalize, lumping together the different genres he has written in to make pronouncements on his language. Thus, whatever defence Macebuh (1988:203) puts forward for Soyinka's "mythic imagination", his work is flawed by overgeneralization which made him to comment thus: "language in Soyinka is difficult, harsh, sometimes tortured; his syntax is often archaic, his verbal structures sometimes impenetrable."

We are not denying the existence of problems in Soyinka's plays or dramaturgy. In fact, myriad problems exist, some of which have been identified in the course of our analysis and which several critics have made notes of. Margaret Laurence's (1968) metaphor of Soyinka spinning so many valuable plates in the air at the same time is a double-edged observation: It is a commendation that indicates the source of real problems in

Soyinka's plays. The sparse production of the major plays in the absence of daring theatre directors like Dapo Adelugba and Femi Osofisan is itself a testimony to the reality of such problems.

However, when the chips are down, Soyinka's theory of ritual drama and its widely encompassing scope has given a major boost to contemporary African drama and has placed him on the same pedestal with world masters of the trade. The contemporary theatre seems to have forgotten that it has its roots in ritual and song, and it is only the rare emergence of a Lorca or a Brecht, or a Wole Soyinka that creates an awareness of our deprivation. (Yankowitz (1966:129)

Cook (1977:117) has sagely observed that, "only a small man tries desperately to assert his own individuality by deliberately shutting himself off from outside influence," Soyinka looms larger than a small man, armed with the ritual aesthetics of his metaphysical milieu and its traditional festivals, he eclectically assembled sundry theatrical histrionics from the Western landscape to create intellectually and aesthetically satisfying plays using ritual as metaphysical, communication and aesthetic strategy to address varied relevant themes. I think what our endeavour, so far, has proved is the assertion by Ann B. Davis to the effect that Soyinka has developed:

> an approach to drama which does not focus exclusively on tragedy, utilizes an inclusive concept of ritual, and treats a broad range of social and psychological processes within the dramatic experience.

The second part of this book examines the links between the concepts of creativity, violence and social commitment in the two novels of Wole Soyinka, *The Interpreters* and *Season of Anomy*. Soyinka's pre-occupation as an artist develops from a metaphysical insight which accounts for his belief that creativity and violence, both attributes of his creative muse, Ogun, are inherent in human nature. He therefore seeks to assume through his literary and political life the role of a warrior in campaign against those things that could give vent to violence in human societies as well as prognosticate about society's rebirth after occasional eruptions of violence. This trend is recognizable in the two texts.

The Interpreters justifies the saying that a writer does not write or create in a vacuum. The work takes a cursory look at post-independence Nigerian society. Soyinka takes the responsibility – as a result of his social commitment – of assessing the values of the various individuals left in the society after the departure of the white colonial masters. However, the picture he finds is not a 'technicolour idyll' to use the words of Chinua Achebe. Those in the upper echelons of the society like Sir Demorin, Chief Winsala and Egbo's grandfather are depicted as corrupt. The group that finds itself in the middle-class, "the interpreters" is to a large extent impotent. The masses from both the rural and urban areas are disenchanted as seen in the reaction to Noah who barely escapes lynching or in the mid-night sentimental visit of Dehinwa's relatives. All in all, corruption, violence, hypocrisy and confusion of values have become common features of the society. Believing the fact that this dark vision cannot continue to prevail, this work is likeable to Soyinka's prediction of the social strife that engulfed the country.

Season of Anomy, Soyinka's second novel depicts a new generation of interpreters in an active struggle to free their society from the unbearable social conditions created by monopoly capitalism and exploitation. The novel bears conspicuous traits of *The Man Died,* the writer's prison notes published earlier on in 1972 and it mirrors the harrowing experience of individuals and the Nigerian society at large during the civil war. It reveals the outcome of the growing societal breakdown described in *The Interpreters* and also portrays the kind of secularized socio-philosophical system which could be achieved in a society after occasional violence or war.

There is a clear interconnection and progression in the thematic concerns of both novels in tune with the mood and level of commitment of Soyinka at the different periods when the works were written. Initially employing *The Interpreters* to satirize the Nigerian post-colonial situation, he moves on to militant writing in *Season of Anomy* in consonance with his defiant mood and personal experience during the period of crisis in Nigeria. The sense of humiliation, isolation and objection as well as his exposure to the intricacies of the grand conspiracy of military rulers, the traditional rulers and the bourgeoisie evoked in him the need for his avowal to militancy and non-compromise after his release from detention. In fact, this led to the emergence of the "anjonu" personality in him.

A dialectical synthesis of the "anjonu" metaphor and the Ogunnian personality originally abiding in him accounts for his social vision in *Season of Anomy*. Thus, instead of mere satirization of the society as it happens in *The Interpreters* or an exposure of the emerging dictatorship in African politics as in his 1967 play *Kongi's Harvest*, he carries the battle in *Season of Anomy* to the "self-consolidating, regurgitative, lumpen mafiadom of the military, the old politicians and business enterprise ..."

Soyinka's characterization moved away from the passive interpreters and corrupt members of the traditional African society in his first novel to the active socially committed characters like Ofeyi and Demakin who both display the attributes of Ogun in the novel. Again, he projects the kind of society he envisions in Aiyero where the people betray an attachment to a communal ideology which socio-mythical affirmations and knowledge of the past strengthen. In terms of aesthetics, Soyinka employs language, setting and plot structure to depict contemporary realities in his works. Myth as seen in both works is dialectically employed by the writer to reinforce the message that the past and the present are inter-linked. The myths provide us in generalized form with the necessary precedent for the examination of our present situation. The adaptations which Soyinka makes in presenting these related myths are combined, drawing our attention to the writer's specific points in *The Interpreters* and *Season of Anomy*.

In conclusion, this work has shown that ritual and social transformations are essentially inter-related. It has also made it clear that Soyinka's commitment emerges out of his understanding of the metaphysics of human nature, demonstrating that revolutionary violence breeds creativity and regeneration. The work has shown Soyinka's social vision and worldview as totally African where the word African itself is taken as dynamic and complexly related to realities in other parts of the world.

INDEX